INDIAN WISDOM
AND
INTERNATIONAL PEACE

INDIAN WISDOM
AND
INTERNATIONAL PEACE

[FROM THE VEDAS & LORD SHRIKRISHNA TO
EX-PRIME MINISTER MORARJI DESAI
WITH
SUPPLEMENTARY WESTERN THOUGHTS]

DR. R.N. VYAS
M.A., PH.D., D. LITT, S.R.

GIAN PUBLISHIHG HOUSE
DELHI-110007

GIAN PUBLISHING HOUSE
29/6 SHAKTI NAGAR, DELHI-110 007

ISBN 81-212-0118-7

PRINTED IN INDIA

Published by Gian Publishing House, Delhi-110007
and Printed at Suman Printers, Delhi-110053

MĀTĀ BHŪMIḤ PUTRO AHAṀ PṚTHIVYAḤ

—Atharva Veda

Eerth is my mother. I am the son of the Earth.

NAMO MĀTRE PṚTHIVYAI NAMO MĀTRE PṚTHIVYAI

—Yajurveda

I bow to mother Earth. I bow to Mother Earth.

MITRASYA CHAKṢUŚĀ ṢAMĪKṢĀMAHE

—Yajurveda

May I see the world with friendly eyes.

PREFACE

Every sensible person should realize the basic importance of World Peace for the survival of mankind. The talk about the necessity of World Peace does not mean indulging in any religious, old-fashioned and meaningless platitude. Atomic weapons have presented a real threat of annihilation to mankind. It has been estimated that our modern world has already manufactured more than twenty thousand megaton atom bombs, while only one hundred megaton atom bombs are sufficient to reduce this earth to ashes.

It is the height of human foolishness that it is wasting that money on preparing weapons of human destruction, which should be used for the betterment of human happiness and reconstruction. Three-fourth of mankind is still living in a very pitiable condition. Millions of people are still half-clad and half-fed. The problems of poverty and ill-health are so widespread that they need human effort lasting for at least one hundred years even in this age of scientific advancement to solve them. Merely a chanting of terms like democracy and communism cannot bring concrete relief to mankind. And yet, people all over the world are being misled in the names of blind nationalism and irrational religion to prepare for the sepulture of humanity.

It is pathetic that despite many nuclear accidents, the

CONTENTS

CHAPTER 1

INTRODUCTION

THE PROBLEM of International Peace is no more the sole concern of the professional politicians. Nor can the intelligent people afford to rest content by handing over the problem of international peace to them and the governments managed and controlled by them. The reason for this fact lies in the invention of the most deadly and devastating weapons which are threatening the very existence of human species.

Modern man has definitely achieved remarkable success in the domain of scientific pursuits. He has visited the surface of the moon and hopes to land on the surface of the Venus. We all know how the man can penetrate the depth of waters, how the man can move faster than sound in the air, how the man can walk across the waters, how the man can transplant the heart and even head. We need not recount the manifold achievements of man here. When we talk about these human achievements, our hearts are filled with rare optimism, rare pride for mankind. But the very next moment when we reflect a little we realize that man has in his zest for inventions and equally strong zest for establishing mastery over the distant lands of the earth and a strong desire to rule other nations and peoples has brought his doom very near. It appears that he is running fast in the direction of annihilation. Sometimes we wonder whether in the name of progress man is not walking in the direction of biological extinction.

How otherwise shall we explain the multiplication of the various nuclear weapons and instruments of chemical and bactereological warfare? Scientists have invented such terrific weapons that a sensible man shall shudder at the very thought of the destruction that can be showered upon mankind by them. There are H-bombs, Super bombs, incendiary weapons, cluster-bombs, Sharpnel bomb, Smart bomb and a host of other instruments of mass-destruction. The H-bomb is roughly "a thousand times more powerful than the A-bomb" that destroyed Hiroshima and Nagasaki within no time in the Second World War. The Super bomb is supposed to be second only to the H-bomb. It is reported that it has a 4.5 ft diametmer and is 11 ft long." Its weight is 15,000 lbs. It contains 12,000 lbs of 'a very powerful explosive of an aquecus get of ammonium nitrate and aluminium powder with an intermediary agent.' This bomb explodes just before touching the ground and explosion can wipe out trees and other obstacles. Its effect is so extensive that it can destroy all animals, plant and human life within a radius of 3200 ft.

'Incendiary bombs like Napalm (900 deg. C. to 1000 deg. C.), Napalm pyrogel and Super weapons (1300 deg. C. to 2000 deg. C.), white phosphorous and thermite (2000 deg. C. to 3000 deg. C.) and magnesium (3000 deg. C. to 3900 deg. C.) are also very destructive in nature. They spread out sticky materials on the body of the victims, which starts burning and penetrates into the flesh. Phosphorous is also very dangerous because either it kills outright or it poisons the liver and attacks kidneys and the nervous system. The survivors offer a picture of crooked bones, molten flesh and stunted limb.

There is another class of bombs called the cluster-bombs. This type of bomb is a "Mother bomb" containing several daughter bombs. The bomb unfolds itself at an altitude of 800 to 1200 metres above the ground and scatters the 'daughter bombs' over a large area. These bombs contain pineapple-like bombs each weighing about 800 grams and containing 260 metal balls of 6.5 cum. diameter. These balls pierce the flesh and muitilate the victims.

Sharpnel Bombs are fired by canons. When they explode, they shoot out 104 small bombs of 2.7 cums. diameter. Each bomb explodes at the height of an average person and projects small fragments towards neck, head and chest of the victims.

The American periodicals *Newsweek* and *Time* reported that American armies used Smart Bombs in their fight against the North Vietnam. These bombs are very accurate shooters. They are of two types. One type of smart bombs are guided by television and the other by Laser beams. The first type of smart bombs weigh more than 3,000 lbs each and can be dropped from a height of 30,000 ft far above the reach of most anti-aircraft guns. What is worth nothing is that the pilot can adjust its course by remote control by seeing its path on television receiver or even the bomb 'having memorized the picture of the target with its built-in electronic brain' can strike accurately. Laser-directed bombs have coordination of about two aircraft. One plane circles above and trains a beam of laser on the target while the other plane drops the bomb in the direction of the target. Following the infrared sensors mounted in their noses, the bomb rides the reflected laser beam to hit the target.

The 'H-bomb' is, really speaking, an amazingly destructive weapon in the armoury of the big nations. Its explosion proceeds in three stages. There is first of all a supply of U235 in the H-bomb. The heat generated by the fission is so intense that it is sufficient to cause the fusion of a supply of hydrogen into helium. Both the U235 and the hydrogen are covered by a thick shell of ordinary uranium. The heat produced by the fusion of hydrogen into helium is strong enough to explode the ordinary uranium in the outer shell. The outer shell of the H-bomb is responsible for most of the energy released by the H-bomb at the time of its explosion. The explosion is marked by the splitting of the uranium atoms into lighter atoms of various kinds which are radio-active in nature.

But this description of the H-bomb cannot give the readers any idea about its capacity of destruction. To say that the destruction caused by the H-bomb is very extensive may not mean much to a reader. But he shall probably get an idea about the destructive capacity of the H-bomb when we recall that Dr. Linus Pauling and other topmost Scientists of the world 9,235 in number addressed a petition as back as January 1958 to Mr. Hammarskjold, then Secretary-General of the U.N.O., to abolish these weapons of mass destruction. Their petition stated:

"We, the scientists whose names are signed below, urge that an international agreement to stop the testing of nuclear bombs be made now.

"Each nuclear bomb test spreads an added burden of radioactive elements over every part of the world. Each added amount of radiation causes damage to the health of human beings all over the world and causes damage to the pool of human germ plasm such as to lead to an increase in the number of seriously defective children that will be born in future generations..."

"We have in common with our fellow men a deep concern for the welfare of all human beings. As scientists, we have knowledge of the dangers involved and therefore a special responsibility to make those dangers known..."

Indian Government published a work named *Nuclear Explosions and their Effects* in 1956. It gives a very objective account of the disastrous effects of the nuclear weapons.

Bertrand Russell stated in his press conference held on July 5 of the year 1955 organized by the *observer*:

"The general public, and even many men in positions of authority, have not realized what would be involved in a war with nuclear bombs. The general public still thinks in terms of the obliteration of cities. It is understood that the new bombs are more powerful than the old, and that, while one A-bomb could obliterate Hiroshima, one H-bomb could obliterate the largest cities, such as London, New York and Moscow."

"No doubt in an H-bomb war great cities would be obliterated. But this is one of the minor disasters that would have to be faced. If everybody in London, New York and Moscow were exterminated the world might, in the course of a few centuries, recover from the blow. But we now know, especially since the *Bikini* test, that nuclear bombs can gradually spread destruction over a very much wider area than had been supposed.

"It is stated on very good authority that a bomb can now be manufactured which will be 2,500 times as powerful as that which destroyed Hiroshima. Such a bomb, if exploded near the ground or under water, sends radioactive particles into the upper air. They sink gradually and reach the surface of the earth in the form of a deadly dust or rain. It was this dust which infected the Japanese fishermen and their catch of fish.

"No one knows how widely such lethal radio-active particles might be diffused, but the best authorities are unanimous in saying that a war with H-bombs might quite possibly put an end to the human race. It is feared that if many H-bombs are used there will be universal death-sudden only for a minority, but for the majority a slow torture of desease and disintegration."

The same type of opinion comes from another expert Linus Pauling in his article *The Humanist* for March-April, 1961 declares that:

"For six billion dollars—one-twentieth of the amount spent on armaments each year by the nations of the world—enough Cobalt bombs could be built to ensure the death of every person on earth. No matter what sort of protection were to be devised, it is highly unlikely that any human being would remain alive."

This Cobalt bomb is exactly like the H-bomb, except that the outer cover consists of cobalt and not of uranium.

Prof. Oskar Morgenstern in his book *The Question of National Defence*, published by Random House Inc. in 1959 writes in his capacity of a defence expert:

"We try to imagine sometimes, as well as we can, what the thermonuclear destruction would mean. But even writers of fiction have failed to give us a deep impression of the nature and extent of this catastrophe. Perhaps even they cannot truly visualize what it would mean to the survivors to see fifty, eighty, or hundred millions people killed within a few days or hours and tens of million grievously ill, living without hope in hovels amidst poisonous radio-active debris.

We are at present focusing attention on the physical holocaust that a large thermonuclear, atomic war would surely bring to the United States. We recoil from that picture of death and destruction so unbelievably great. Our mind refuses to tell us that life after this war would be possible, or if possible, worth-living. This may very well be so."

It should be noted that the destructive effects of nuclear weapons are not limited to the destruction of human life immediately. They are so dangerous that even the future progeny become subjected to their ruinous effect. A.H. Sturtevant, a distinguished American specialist on the science of heredity has declared:

"There is no possible escape from the conclusion that the bombs already exploded will ultimately result in the production of numerous defective individuals—if the human race itself survives for many generations...I regret that an official (Admiral Strauss) in a position of such responsibility should have stated that there is no biological hazard from low doses of high energy radiation."

The genetic damage shall extend to the distinct generations and thus the entire future humanity shall greatly suffer as a result of mere tests of these nuclear weapons.

Moreover, the question of enormous wastage of money spent on the production of these instruments of human destruction should not be forgotten. Big nations are spending about fifty-five percent of their budget on the production of these instruments of mass butchery. The total amount of money being spent on the production of the war-weapons by the world is really much more exorbitant though David Cushman Coyal in his book *The United Nations and How it Works* states that "the world is spending about 1,20,000 millon dollars per year for military activities". According to Bertrand Russell: "At the present time the nations engaged in the cold war spend on preparations for slaughter thirty thousand million pounds a year, or 570 thousand pounds a minute." I am afraid that the actual expenditure being incurred in the manufacturing of weapons of humanity's death is even more than this because the nations take precaution to hide the actual expenditure of war-weapons and prefer to give false figures to deceive even their own people. This is done by saying that it is not in public interests to place actuality before the people.

It is really shocking to note that such a wanton misuse of money is being made by spending a great bulk of people's hard-earned money on gun powder instead of using it for clothing the naked and for feeding the hungry who need monetary help urgently to save their lives from the torturing death.

This modest detail of the present situation should convince a sensible reader to realize how necessary is it to save humanity from another war. If we therefore talk about peace, it is because of the danger of human destruction that is bound to result from any war of nuclear weapons. It is astonishing to note that people are being duped by a mischievous doctrine that the war is rooted in human nature. Scientists have very efficiently and conclusively established that the original man did not have any institution of war and that the latter has come into being much later in the life of humanity due to the cupidity of the ruling scoundrels.

For example, W.H.R. Rivers, G. Eliot Smith and W.J. Perry hold that war was invented in pre-dynastic Egypt.[1] Prof. M.F. Ashley Montagu is of the opinion that war came to this world only when man reached the agricultural state of development, 20,000 years ago.[2] Hobhouse, Wheeler and Ginsberg have established that the history of certain primitive tribes has been devoid of any warfare.[3] Pitirim A. Sorokin is also of this very opinion as is clear from his classic work *Reconstruction of Humanity.* B. Malinowski in his work *Freedom and Civilization* has concluded that war does not exist among primitives. A noted English thinker R.G. Collingwood has given his frank opinion in his book *The New Leviathan* to the effect that "the earliest human communities of which we know seem not to have waged war."

Psychologists have given their clear verdict when out of 378 members of the American Psychological Association, 346 (i.e.

1. Vide, Qunicy Wright. *A Study of War,* Vol. 1, p. 34.

2. Vide, Man's Most Dangerous Fallacy: the myth of races—quoted in T.H. Pear (editor), *Psychological Factors of Peace and War,* p. 29.

3. Vide, The Material Culture and Social Institutions of Simpler Peoples.

91 per cent) gave a definite "No" to the question "Do you as a psychologist hold that there are present in human nature ineradicable instinctive factors that make war between nations inevitable ?"

Darwin's theory that struggle and conflict is the law of nature has been proved false by the investigations of Prince Kropotkin who established that not conflict but cooperation is the rule of survival in nature. Even ants cooperate, not to speak about the higher beings and animals. Some psychologists (and they are in a very slender minority) try to prove that "aggression is always a consequence of frustration." The state prepares outlets of pent-up aggression in the form of war. John Dollard Leonard, W. Doob and others have tried to establish this in a work entitled *Frustration and Aggression.* But even this view is untenable because even if we grant for the sake of argument that frustration in a man leads to aggression, it does not imply that the war is the only outlet of this aggression. We can find out even other channels to frustration. In fact with proper education, man can be taught to choose a better medium of expressing his frustration.

Even the Marxian theory of inevitable conflict between the haves and havenots has been found defective. Marxists believe that the exploitation of labour leads to a shrinkage of domestic market with the result that the capitalists try to grab new markets and sources of raw materials outside their country. The result is war. Capitalist imperialism always breeds war.

The fact is that there is nothing in human nature which must lead men to wage bloody wars. Had man been so constituted, the state departments would not have been required to constitute Recruitment Offices and the soldiers would not have run away from the battlefields. In fact our world would have been filled with soldiers on all sides. What is still more significant, there would not have been the cult of pacifists, for who can go against the inherent nature ? Hence, we must conclude that there is no scientific ground for presuming that war is rooted in human nature. The traditional idea that war is ineradicable as it is rooted in human nature is as unscientific in nature as the idea that Rahu davours the Sun and this causes the solar eclipse or to think that the Sun moves around the earth. Our unreflective attitude has done much harm to humanity so far as the institution of the war is concerned. People have been taught this lesson by the persons enjoying political power and pelf that war is inevitable, no, a pious thing that must be eulogised and extolled. The result is that the bulk of mankind has accepted war as rooted in human nature. Our traditionally written histories, literature and works of religion have only tried to drive this very thing in the minds of people all the more.

Unfortunately some scientists like Darwin, McDougall and Freud consciously or unconsciously gave some scientific prop to the unreflective mind. Darwin preached that the nature wants that there should be a struggle for the survival in which the strongest invariably wins. In fact Darwin's theory was not based on any scientific observation. He was influenced by the might of the British nation that was the strongest nation of the world at the time of Darwin. McDougall, another British scientist, postulated the theory of instincts. He was of the opinion that the instinct of pugnacity, which expresses itself in aggression is rooted in human nature. The whole theory of instincts has been found untenable by the subsequent psychologists. But even if the instinct of pugnacity is accepted, McDougall himself has stated that the instincts are malleable in nature. It means that we can transform them in an entirely new shape. Thus sex-instinct has been transformed in the institution of marriage. If this is the case, then even the instinct of pugnacity can be transformed into something sociable like a tendency of opposing what is against the interests of human society or fight against social evils like inequality, poverty, backwardness.

Freud in his later writings declared that there is an underived aggressive instinct called Thanatos in man.[1] According to him, Thanatos is an impulse to destroy. But at the same time he postulated an instinct of love which he named Fros. Both these impulses are opposite in nature. When there is unbalance between these impulses, it results in the overactivity of Thanatos and the result is aggression. This aggression may turn inwards and take the form of suicide; or it may

1. Vide, *Psychological Factors of Peace and War*, edited by T.H. Pear, 1950, p. 162.

turn outwards and may be expressed in the form of outward aggression.

But this theory of Freud itself is based upon his experience of unbalanced persons. Freud usually came in contact with only abnormal personalities as he was concerned with curing mental ailments. His observations, moreover, is smack of imagination rather than actuality. But even if for argument's sake we concede the existence of Thanatos, we should not forget that Freud believes in the sublimation of the basic human urges. That means that even Thanatos can be sublimated. And even if both these urges i.e. Thanatos and Eros are accepted we can strengthen Eros and weaken Thanatos through sublimation. The total result is that the impulse of aggression need not remain in the present form.

A modern American psychologist Bruno Bettleheim has echoed Freud correctly when he states that "violence exists, surely, and each of us is born with his potential for it. But we are also born with opposite tendencies, and these must be carefully nurtured if we are to counterbalance the violence." Does it not imply that aggression even if inborn, can be eliminated ? Or if it cannot be eliminated, can it not be reduced, weakened and modified to such an extent that it will cease to be a source of danger to the human world ?

Even if we accept for a moment that man is basically a violent animal, our modern scientific mind which can even change the *genes* and can control the environment to a great extent, can do something to transform the violent animal into a peaceful being. If a tiger can be tamed, why can we not tame a man who is definitely much less ferocious than any wild animal by nature ?

In the end I shall like to conclude with the words of Thoreau:

"If I seem to boast more than is becoming, my excuse is that I brag for humanity rather than for myself; and my shortcomings and inconsistencies do not affect the truth of my statement. Notwithstanding much cant and hypocracy-chaff which I find it difficult to separate from my wheat but for which I am as sorry as any man—I will breathe freely and stretch myself in this respect, it is such a relief to both the moral and physical system; and I am resolved that I will not through humility become the devil's attorney. I will endeavour to speak a good word for the truth."

Again it is my duty to invite the attention of my readers to the poignant truth pointed by Thoreau:

"The mass of them (people) serve the State thus; not as men mainly, but as machines, with their bodies. They are the standing army and the militia, jailors, constables, posse comitatus etc... In most cases there is no free exercise whatever of the judgement or the moral sense, but they put themselves on a level with wood and earth and stones; and wooden men can perhaps be manufactured that will serve the purpose as well. Such commands no more respect than men of straw or a lump of dirt. They have the same sort of worth only as horses and dogs."

It is our duty as such to try our utmost to stop states from murdering mankind. The sooner it is done, the better it is.

CHAPTER 2

THE BASIS OF PEACE

(A) MISCELLANY OF INDIAN THOUGHT FROM THE VEDAS, SMRITIS AND SAINTS

THE VEDAS occupy a very important and unique position in the history and culture of India. The Rigveda happens to be the oldest piece of literature of not only India but even of the world.

Technically the Mantra and the Brahmana portions are termed as the Vedas (mantrabrahmanayorvedanamadheyam). The Vedas are four in number viz. the Rig, Saman, Yajur and Atharva. They have the subdivisions of Brahamanas, which are the works of rituals, and the Aranyakas and the Upanishads, which are full of philosophical wisdom of the highest type. Though the Vedas are the oldest works, they contain some of the most significant and important truth about social philosophy. The keynote of the Vedic thought is conveyed by the statement:

"May all the beings see me as a friend and may I see all the beings as my friends."

Buddhism and Jainism too are the product of the Vedic Thought, because the latter is in fact a treasure house of many noble ideas. People differ in their tendencies and therefore they accept only those thoughts which are in keeping with their mental constitution. Therefore Buddhism gave supreme importance to non-violence and Jainism gave supreme importance to austerity. But these both love universal peace like the Vedas. For example look to the 'Metta Sutta' of Buddhism which states:

Whatever living beings there be...
May all beings be happy.
Let none deceive another
Nor despise any person whatsoever in any place.
Let him not wish any harm to another
Out of anger or ill will.
Just as a mother would protect her only child
At the risk of her own life
Even so let him cultivate a boundless heart
Towards all beings.
Let his thoughts of boundless love
Pervade the whole world,
Above, below, and across without any obstruction
Without any hatred, without any enmity.
Whether he stands, walks, sits,
Lies down, as long as he is awake
He should develop his mindfulness—
This they say is the noblest living here.

Like Buddhism, Jainism too loves non-violence. There is a very sublime thought behind this spirit of non-violence. To harm others is in fact to harm oneself.

"Thou art he whom thou intendest to kill. Thou art he whom thou intendest to tyrannize over."

The *Smriiies* occupy a place of pride in the pattern of Hindu society. Hindu religion follows the dictates of the Shrutis, Smritis and Puranas (Shruti-Smriti-puranokta). Smritis are the guides to actual conduct. The key-note of the Smritis is to make one's conduct so sublime in this nation that it may act as a model to every other nation, and person.

(etaddesha prasutasya sakashadagrajanmanah svam svam charitram shiksherana prithivyam sarva manavah.)

Thus we find that Indian thought right from its beginning loves universal fraternity and peace. This very feeling has found an expression in India's policy of universal amity and peaceful coexistence.

Let me quote Smt. Indira Gandhi, the late Prime Minister of India to prove my point.

"Nationalism does not detach us from our common humanity... Our world is small but it has room for all of us to live together and to improve the quality of the lives for our peoples in peace and beauty."

VEDIC LITERATURE

O ye mankind, let all your activities lead you to one common goal (for which) let there be a common language for all of you and let your mind be all of one accord to acquire the knowledge of various sciences fully and like the enlightened seers who lived before you, you ought to worship me alone Who am the only real object of your devotion.

O ye mankind, let the object of your thought be the same, the place of your assembly ought to be common, your mind should be of one accord and let your hearts be united together; I initiate you in the common inspired hymn and provide all of you with common objects for accepting and offering.

O ye mankind, let your object of life be one and the same, let your hearts be equal (in feeling) and let your minds be united together so that there may be an excellent common status of life for all. —*Rigveda Mandala* X, adhyaya 12, Sukta 191

Let all these (men) who are brothers (to one another) advance forward unitedly for the attainment of prosperity, for there is none high or low (amongst them). The Most Exalted Ordainer (of the universe), and the Just Divinity is their Father. Let the earth pouring forth abundant milk etc. bring auspicious days for the living creatures. —*Rigveda*, V-60-5

May all the learned men be friendly to us, may the holy words (of the sagacious) with their pure thoughts be the source of universal peace and happiness. May the liberal ones and those who have taken the vow of serving all living beings be the promoters of general welfare and may all the heavenly objects together with the creatures which dwell on earth and in waters be helpful to our noble undertakings. —*Rigveda*, VII-35-11

May the night and dawn be sweet for us and may every atom of the earth be full of sweetness and may the protecting light of the Sun be sweet. —*Rigveda*, I-90-7

Let the rich satisfy the powerless poor who are in need of means of subsistence and let him think over the long pathway (of the worldly ups and downs). Riches roll like the wheels of the chariot now it comes to one man and then it goes to another. —*Rigveda*, X-117-5

O ye enlightened persons, you are fit for our association, may we (in your company) ever hear with our ears such words which are beneficial (to all) and we ever see with our eyes whatever is good. Ever praying with our firm limbs, may we attain such state of life through our bodies which will be helpful to the cause of the enlightened persons. —*Yajurveda* 25-21

O ye mankind, who are respectful to elders possessing noble hearts, friendly in your undertakings of acquiring wealth and walking in the same path bearing the common yoke together, be never disunited with one another. Come, I make you one-intentioned and one-minded. Let each one of you speak sweetly to the other.

Let your place of drinking water be common and let the partaking of your food be together as I join you to a common yoke; worship Agni (The Supreme Lord in the form of Fire) together attaching yourselves to Him just as the spokes are attached to the nave of the chariot from all sides.

I enjoin on you to be mutually helpful, to be united in your mind and to have common ideal of life for benefiting one another; like the enlightened persons who ever take care of the immortal principle (in their lives). May the friendly feelings amongst you increase morning and evening.

—*Atharva Veda*, 3-30 from 2 to 7

May we be fearless of our friends and even of those who are

unfriendly to us, may we never fall in dread of those whom we know and even of those whom we do not know. May we remain free from any apprehension by night and in the day-time, and may all the (beings residing in the various) quarters be friendly to us. —*Atharva Veda*, 19-15-6

May there be peace in the heavenly region, may there be peace in the environment, may peace reign on the earth, may the waters be soothing and may the medicinal herbs be healing; may the plants be the source of peace to all; may all the enlightened persons bring peace to us, may the Vedas spread peace throughout, may all other objects give us peace and may peace even bring peace to all and may that peace come to me (ever). Om, Peace, Peace, Peace. —*Yajurveda*, 36-17

O Lord, the Dispeller of the darkness of ignorance, please make me firm (in my conviction) so that all the living beings may look towards me with the eye of a friend. And may I also look towards all living beings with the eye of a friend. May we look towards one another (ever) with the eye of a friend.
—*Yajurveda*, 36-18

May the earth be peaceful, may the atmosphere be peaceful, may the medicinal herbs be peaceful, may all my shining objects be peaceful for me, may all the enlightened persons be peaceful for me, may all the peaceful actions be peaceful by means of peace. By the peace may we alleviate that which is terrific here, that which is cruel here, that which is sin here. Let all these be calmed and made auspicious. Let all be gracious unto us.
—*Atharva Veda*, 19-1-9

O ye mankind, I ordain for you to have concordance in your heart, unanimity in your minds and freedom from hatred in your dealings. Everyone of you ought to love one another in every way, just as the inviolable cow loveth the calf which is born from her. —*Atharva Veda*, 3-30-1

Human Debt :

Verily, whoever exists, he, in being born, is born due to a debt to the gods, to the Rishis, to the parents, and to men. For, inasmuch as he is bound to worship, for that reason he is born due to a debt to the gods. Therefore when he worships them, he does so by way of discharging his debt to the gods. And still further inasmuch as he is bound to study for that reason he is born because of his debt to the Rishis. Therefore it is to them that he repays his debt. One who has made proper study, they call him 'the treasure-custodian of the Rishis.'

And further, inasmuch as, he is bound to wish for offspring, for that reason, he is born due to a debt to the parents. Therefore when he provides a continuous and uninterrupted lineage, he does so to repay his debt to his forefathers. And further, inasmuch as he is bound to practise hospitability, he does so because he owes a debt to humanity. It is by way of discharging this debt that he does so. Whosoever performs these duties, fulfils his obligation. By him all is sustained, all is conquered.

—*Shatapatha Brahmana*, 1-7-2

"The Infinite is the source of joy. There is no joy in the finite. Only in the Infinite is there joy. Ask to know of the Infinite.'
'Sir, I wish to know of it.'

'Where one sees nothing but the One, hears nothing but the One, knows nothing but the One—there is Infinite. Where one sees another, hears another, knows another—there is the finite. The Infinite is immortal, the finite is mortal.'

'In what does the Infinite rest ?'

'In its own glory, nay, not even in that. In the world it is said that cows and horses, elephants and gold, slaves, wives, fields, and houses are man's glory—but these are poor and finite things. How shall the Infinite rest anywhere but in itself ? 'The Infinite is below, above, behind, before, to the right, to the left. I am all this. This Infinite is the Self. The Self is below, above, behind, before, to the right, to the left. I am all this. One who knows, meditates upon, and realizes the truth of the Self—such as one delights in the Self, reveals in the Self, rejoices in the Self. He becomes master of himself, and master of all the worlds. Slaves are they who know not this truth.'

—*Chhandogya Upanishad*, VII, 23,24,25

Now we point out the common duty of the followers of all the *ashramas*. It consists in abstaining from violence of every type. One should not harm any being whatsoever. One should always speak the truth, irrespective of the profit or loss resulting therefrom. One should not swerve from the path of truthfulness in any circumstance. One should be free from the blemishes One should be kind to all. One should have the habit of forgiving all. These things are the common duties of people belonging to any as harma of life. —*Pulusta Smriti*, 22

A householder should be compassionate to all. He should be patient towards everybody. He should be free from envy. He should be devoid of impurity of mind and heart. He should always strive for the welfare of humanity. He should be free from avarice. And he should not have any trace of evil desires or aspirations. —*Buddha Smriti*

There is no higher religion than doing good to others; and there is no irreligion worse than harming a person.

—*Ramacharita Manasa* of TULASIDAS

A true God-lover is he who cares for the torments of others, who constantly serves others without any sense of pride, who respects the entire world and never indulges in the censure of anybody and is pure in speech, body and mind.

—NARASI MEHATA

Hear, O Human brothers, man is the foremost truth. There is no truth beyond that. —CHANDIDASA

BUDDHISM

A feeling of Friendliness :

It is the duty of a person wishing peacefulness and expert in attaining the betterment of the Self to be tolerant, exceedingly simple, sweet-tongued, kind-hearted and free from a trace of the ego.

One should not indulge in any mean act that may give good persons an opportunity of finding fault with us. We should always entertain this feeling in the part of our hearts that may all beings of the world be happy, healthy and full of bliss. May all the beings whether they are moveable or inert, big or small, visible or invisible, close to us or far from us, be felicitious.

May we not deceive each other, may we not insult each other; may we not think of harming others out of envy or peevishness. Just as a mother maintains her darling son even at the cost of her life, in the similar way, we should express immeasurable affection for all the beings.

We should build a lofty feeling of friendliness, free from any trace of enmity or bitterness, above and below, in all the four quarters, for all the beings.

We should keep a constant memory of this friendliness, whether we are standing, walking, sitting, or lying, till the time we are lost in the embrace of sleep.

This condition of our life has been described as outward life in this world. Only that man can disseminate a feeling of universal friendship in all four quarters whose mind has become devoid of the tendencies of avarice, enmity and attachment. He showers with friendly disposition the pleasant rains of love on all the beings residing in the four quarters. He gains the excellent fruit of the feelings of compassion, happiness, and non-attachment without any effort whatsoever.

—Metta Sutta and Kalama Sutta

Freedom from Anger:

The impulse of enmity of those persons is never quietened who make it point to retain ideas like, 'That person has abused me; That person has beaten me; That person has vanquished me; That person has looted me," in their minds, and intend to take retaliation.

Inimical feelings disappear only from the minds of those persons who harbour thoughts like, 'I have been abused by that fellow; That fellow has hit me; That fellow has defeated me; That fellow has plundered me' out of their minds and hearts. Enmity can never be pacified by enmity. Enmity can be pacified only by love. This is an eternal law.

—Yamaka Vaggo, Dhammapada

Those who think: 'Let ours indulge in conflict; but we are determined to keep ourselves away from conflict' are able to destroy their sense of enmity, envy and conflict.

Why cannot there be any unity and fellow-feeling amongst

you when unity can be found even in the breakers of human bones, murderers, thieves of cows, horses, and riches etc. and the persons setting a nation on fire ?

—*Upakkilesa, Suttanta, Majjhima Nikaya*

Jaina Oath:

O God, I take the oath of not harming any being whatsoever. I shall never harm or kill the beings whether they are small or big, moveable or immoveable. Nor shall I get them killed. Nor shall I support anybody harming or killing them. O God, I shall keep myself aloof mentally, bodily and orally from such violence. I hereby condemn this sin and censure it strongly. I undertake to keep myself quite unaffected by this spirit of violence. —*Acharanga Sutra*

"All that we are is the result of what we have thought; it is founded on our thoughts, it is made up of our thoughts. If a man speaks or acts with an evil thought, pain follows him, as the wheel follows the foot of the ox that draws the carriage."

"All that we are is the result of what we have thought: it is founded on our thoughts, it is made up of our thoughts. If a man speaks or acts with a pure thought, happiness follows him, like a shadow that never leaves him."

"Let the wise man guard his thoughts which are difficult to perceive, very artful; they rush wherever they list; thoughts well-guarded bring happiness." —*Dhammapada*.

(B) PHILOSOPHY OF THE INFINITE

The main source of any nation's central thought is its principal philosophical thought. This is true in the case of India to a great extent. The basic philosophical thought of India is found in the Upanishads, which are the most important parts of the Vedas. The Upanishadic thought is so important that it has influenced all subsequent Indian minds directly or indirectly. While I will not like to present the whole picture of the Upanishadic thought, because that is the subject matter of Philosophy, I shall like to present that aspect of the Upanishads that is significant from the standpoint of idea of international peace.

The Supreme Reality according to the Upanishads is Brahman. The very word Brahman means the biggest conceivable reality. Shankara states in his Brahma Sutra Bhashya 2-1-14 "Modifications or effects are names only, exist through or originate from speech only, while in reality there exists no such things as a modification...So this manifold world with its objects of enjoyment, enjoyers and so on has no existence apart from the Brahman." Still further, an analogy has been given to explain the point. "The sea in itself is one, but manifold as having waves and foam; so the clay in itself is one, but manifold if viewed withr egard to the jars and dishes made of it."

Aldous Huxley rightly calls this Brahman as 'the integrating principle of all being.'

The Isha Upanishad states: "In the heart of all things, of whatever there is in the universe, dwells the Lord." (*Isha*-1)

The Kena Upanishad states "This ist he truth of Brahman in relation to nature; whether in the flash of the lightning, or in the wink of the eyes, the power that is shown is the power of Brahman" (IV.4)

"This is the truth of Brahman in relation to men: in the motions of the mind, the power that is shown is the power of Brahman." (IV.5)

The Mundaka Upanishad states : "The Imperishable is the Real. As sparks innumerable fly upward from a blazing fire, so from the depths of the Imperishable arise all things. To the depths of the Imperishable they again descend. Self-luminous is that Being, and formless. He dwells within all and without all. He is unborn, pure, greater than the greatest, without breath, without mind.

From Him are born breath, mind, the organs of sense, ether, air, fire, water, and the earth, and He binds all these together.

Heaven is His head, the Sun and the moon his eyes, the four quarters His ears, the revealed scriptures His voice, the air His breath, the universe His heart. From His feet came the earth. He is the innermost Self of all." (II.i.1-4)

Again that very Upanishad adds:

"Self-luminous is Brahman, ever present in the hearts of all.

He is the refuge of all, He is the supreme goal. In Him exists all that moves and breathes. In Him exists all that is, He is both that which is gross and that which is subtle. Adorable is He. Beyond the ken of the senses is He. Supreme is He. Attain thou Him.

He, the self-luminous, subtler than the subtlest, in Whom exist all the worlds and all those that live therein—He is the Imperishable Brahman. He is the principle of life. He is speech, and He is mind. He is real. He is immortal. Atttain Him, O my friend, the one goal to be attained." (*Ibid.*, ii.1-2)

The Shvetashvatara Upanishad identifies the Brahman with the universe adding significant statements 'yet He is still the same.'

Thou art the fire,
Thou art the Sun,
Thou art the air,
Thou art the moon,
Thou art the starry firmament,
Thou art Brahman Supreme,
Thou art the waters-thou
the creator of all.
Thou art woman, Thou art man,
Thou art the youth, Thou art the maiden,
Thou art the old man tottering with his staff;
Thou facest everywhere,
Thou art the dark butterfly,
Thou art the green parrot with red eyes,
Thou art the thunder cloud, the seasons, the seas.
Without beginning art Thou,
Beyond time, beyond space,
Thou art He from whom sprang
The three worlds.' (IV. 2-4)

Then there is the famous Peace chant stating:

Filled with Brahman are the things we see;
Filled with Brahman are the things we see not;
From out of Brahman floweth all that is;
From Brahman all-yet is He still the same.

The Upanishadic teaching is against any multiplicity. The

famous thinker of the Brihadaranyaka states: "As long as there is duality, one sees the other, one hears the other, one smells the other, one speaks to the other, one thinks of the other, one knows the other; but when for the illumined soul the all is dissolved in the Self, who is there to be seen by whom, who is there to be smelt by whom, who is there to be heard by whom, who is there to be spoken by whom, who is there to be thought by whom, who is there to be known by whom ? Ah, Maitreyi, my beloved, the Intelligence which reveals all—by what shall it be revealed ? By whom shall the Knower be known ? The Self is described as not this, not that. It is incomprehensible, for it cannot be comprehended; undecaying, for it never decays; unattached, for it never attaches itself; unbound, for it is never bound. By whom, O my beloved, shall the Knower be known ?' (IV.v. 14-15)

Shri Ramakrishna, who had realized the truth about the Ultimate Reality has explained this thing in a very lucid way. He states :

"But the vijnani, who gains an intimate knowledge of Brahman has his consciousness further extended. He knows that roof and steps are all of the same substance. First he realizes, 'All is not, God is'. Next he realizes, 'All is God.' Few can stay long on the roof Those who reach samadhi and attain Brahman soon return to the normal plane of consciousness, and then they realize that He has become everything. They then see God in the heart of all."

(*Shri Ramakrishna Kathamritha*, vol. III, pp. 11-12)

The Chandogya Upanishad tells us that an individual is essentially immortal Self.

"This body is mortal, always gripped by death, but within it dwells the immortal Self. This Self, when associated in our consciousness with the body, is subject to pleasure and pain; and so long as this association continues, freedom from pleasure and pain can no man find. But as this association ceases, there cease also the pleasure and the pain. Rising above physical consciousness, knowing the Self to be distinct from the senses and the mindknowing it in its true light—one rejoices and is free."

(xii.1)

Therefore one is the Atman, one is Brahman, as the Atman and the Brahman are the names of one sole substance.

This fact is conveyed by the famous statement "That art Thou".

Let us follow this dialogue:

"Please, sir, tell me more about this Self."

'Be it so, my son.'

'The rivers in the east flow eastward, the rivers in the west flow westward, and all enter into the sea. From sea to sea they pass, the clouds lifting them to the sky as vapour and sending them down as rain. And these rivers, when they are united with the sea, do not know whether they are this or that river, likewise all those creatures that I have named, when they have come back from Brahman, know not whence they came.'

'All those beings have their self in Him alone. He is the Truth He is the subtle essence of all. He is the self. And that, Shvetaketu, That art Thou.'

'Please, sir, tell me more about the Self.'

'Be it so my child' (*Chhandogya Upanishad* X)

'If someone were to strike once at the root of this large tree, it would bleed, but live. If he were to strike at its stem, it would bleed, but live. If he were to strike at the top, it would bleed, but live. Pervaded by the living Self, this tree stands firm, and takes its food; but if the Self were to depart from one of its branches, that branch would wither; if it were to depart from a second, that would wither; if it were to depart from the third, that would wither. If it were to depart from the whole tree, the whole tree would wither.'

'Likewise, my son, know this: The body dies when the Self leaves it—but the Self dies not.'

'All that has its self in Him alone. He is truth. He is subtle essence of all. He is the Self. And that, Shveaketu, That art Thou.'

'Please, sir, tell me more about this Self.'

'Be it so. Bring a fruit of that Nyagrodha tree.'

'Here it is, sir.'

'Break it.'

'It is broken, sir.'

'What do you see ?'

'Some seeds, extremely small, sir.'

'Break one of them.'

'It is broken, sir.'

'What do you see ?'

'Nothing, sir.'

'The subtle essence you do not see, and in that is the whole of the Nyagrodha tree. Believe, my son, that which is the subtle essence—in that have all things their existence. That is truth. That is the Self. And that, Shvetaketu, That art Thou.'

'Please, sir, tell me more about this Self.'

'Be it so. Put this salt in water, and come to me tomorrow morning.'

Shvetaketu did as he was bidden. The next morning his father asked him to bring the salt which he had put in the water. But he could not, for it had dissolved. Then said Uddalaka:

'Sip the water, and tell me how it tastes.'

'It is salty, sir.'

'In the same way', continued Uddalaka, 'Though you do not see Brahman in this body, He is indeed here. That which is subtle essence—in that have all beings their existence. That is the truth. That is the Self. And that Shvetaketu, That art Thou.'

'Please, sir, tell me more about this Self,' said the youth again.

'Be it so, my child.'

'As a man may be blindfolded, and led away, and left in a strange place; and as, having been so dealt with, he turns in every direction and cries out for someone to remove his bondages and show him the way home; and as one thus entreated may loose his bandages and give him comfort; and as thereupon he walks home at last—just so does a man who meets with an illumined teacher obtain true knowledge. 'That which is the subtle essence—in that have all beings there existence. That is the truth. That is the Self. And O Shvetaketu, That art Thou.'

'Please, sir, tell me more about this Self.'

'Be it so, my child.'

'When a man is fatally ill, his relations gather round him and ask, "Do you know me ? Do you know me ?" Now until his speech is merged in his mind, his mind in his breath, his breath in his vital heat, his vital heat in the Supreme Being, he knows them. But when his speech is merged in his mind, his mind in his breath, his breath in his vital heat, his vital heat in the Supreme Being, then he does not know them.

'That which is the subtle essence—in that have all beings their existence. That is the truth. That is the Self. And that, O Shvetaketu, That art Thou.' (*Chhandogya*, xi-xv)

The Mundaka Upanishad tells us "The Self is not known by the weak, nor by the thoughtless, nor by those who do not rightly meditate. But by the rightly meditative, the thoughtful, and the strong, He is fully known.' (II.ii, 4)

The Aitareya Aranyaka tells us:

"He who is aware how that Self-gradually unfolds within him obtains for himself a greater development. Herbs and trees and animals he sees, and he knows that in them too the Self is gradually revealed. For in herbs and trees there is only sap, but in animals there is mind. Among animals moreover, it can be seen that the Self is manifested little by little, for in some of them thought is present as well as sap, but in others there is sap only. And in man, especially the Self by degrees unfolds itself, for he of all beings is most endowed with consciousness. He says what he has known, he sees what he has known, he knows what is to happen tomorrow, he know the gross and the subtle. In this mortality he desires the immortal. Thus is he endowed. In other animate beings understanding goes no further than hunger and thirst: they do not say what they have known, nor do they see what they have known. They do not know what is to happen tomorrow, nor do they know the gross and the subtle. To a certain point they go—but they go no further." (II.ii. 1-5)

In the words of Isha Upanishad we can say "At the heart of all—whatever there is in the universe—abides the Self." This

Self is the only reality. Everything is done for the sake of this Self alone.

Yajnavalkya states to his wife in the Brihadaranyaka Upanishad this very truth in a very straightforward manner. It is in the form of a dialogue that deserves to be quoted:

Yajnavalkya : "Maitreyi, I am resolved to renounce the world and begin the life of renunciation, I wish therefore to divide my property between you and my other wife, Katyayani."

Maitreyi: "My lord, if this whole earth belonged to me, with all its wealth, should I through its possession attain immortality ?"

Yajnavalkya: 'No, Your life would be like that of the rich. None can possibly hope to attain immortality through wealth.'

Maitreyi: 'Then what need have I of wealth ? Please, my lord, tell me what you know about the way to immortality.'

Yajnavalkya: 'Dear to me have you always been, Maitreyi, and now you ask to learn of that truth which is nearest to my heart. Come, sit by me. I will explain it to you. Meditate on what I say.'

'It is not for the sake of the busband, my beloved, that the husband is dear, but for the sake of the Self.'

'It is not for the sake of the wife, my beloved, that the wife is dear, but for the sake of the Self.

'It is not for the sake of the children, my beloved, that the children are dear, but for the sake of the Self.'

'It is not for the sake of wealth, my beloved, that wealth is dear, but for the sake of of the Self.' (II.iv. 1-5)

And this Self is Infinite and all pervading.

The Chhandogya Upanishad throws light on the nature of this Infinite.

"The Infinite is the source of joy. There is no joy in the finite. Only in the Infinite is there joy. Ask to know of the Infinite."

'Sir, I wish to know of it.'

'Where one sees nothing but the One, hears nothing but the One, knows nothing but the One—there is the Infinite. Where one sees another, hears another, knows another—there is the finite. The Infinite is immortal, the finite is mortal.'

'In what does the Infinite rest ?'

'In its own glory, nay, not even in that. In the world it is said that cows and horses, elephants and gold, slaves, wives, fields, and houses are man's glory-but these are poor and finite things. How shall infinite rest anywhere but in itself ?

'The Infinite is below, above, behind, before, to the right, to the left. I am all this. This Infinite is the Self. The Self is below, above, behind, before, to the right, to the left. I am all this. One who knows, meditates upon, and realizes the truth of the Self—such an one delights in the Self, reveals in the Self, rejoices in the Self. He becomes master of himself, and master of all the worlds. Slaves are they who know not this truth.'
(VII.23,24,25)

The Katha very categorically states that this very self-appears to be many.

"As the fire, though one, takes the shape of every object which it consumes, so the Self, though one, takes the shape of every object in which it dwells.

As air, though one, takes the shape of every object which it enters, so the Self, though one, takes the shape of every object in which it dwells.

As the Sun, revealer of all objects to the seer, is not harmed by the sinful eye, nor by the impurities of the objects it gazes on, so the one Self, dwelling in all, is not touched by the evils of the world, For he transcends all.

He is one, the lord and innermost Self of all; of one from, he makes of himself many forms. To him who sees the Self revealed in his heart belongs eternal bliss—to none else, to non else." (II.v.9-12)

Thus we find that the Upanishadic philosophy clearly tells that there is no reason to make differentiations that are responsible for conflicts. Truth has to be grasped through supreme knowledge (para vidya). It is admitted that there is difference and distinction on the lower level of life or empirical life. But one has to rise above it. One has to transcend one's ordinary personality which is based on ignorance and defective thinking. One has to exceed one's ordinary Self to realize the truth.

The Upanishads are alive to the fact that this is possible only through systematic supreme-truth-oriented education. This education should begin right from childhood when mind is more receptive and the mental personality is under formation. For example the Mahabharata tells to follow the following maxims:

'Treat others as thou wouldst thyself be treated.'

(*Shanti parva* 167)

'Do nothing to thy neighbour which hereafter thou wouldst not have thy neighbour do to thee.' (Anushasana parva 113.8)

'He who is always a friend of others and by his word, thought, and deed is continually engrossed in doing good to others—he, O Jajali, knows the meaning of dharma.'

(*Shanti parva* 262.9)

'Kindness is desiring happiness for all. Straightforwardness is mental poise. Holy is he who is kind to all. Wicked is he who is cruel.' (*Vana parva* 313.90)

'The secret meaning of the Vedas is truth; of truth, self-control; of self-control, freedom from all limitations. This is the sum of all scriptures.' (*Shanti parva* 251.11)

The Rigveda wishes that our hearts and minds should be united.

'Let your thoughts be one and single,
Let your hearts be joined in one;
Both the mind at rest in union
At peace with all.' (x-129.4)

Therefore the Taittiriya Upanishad tells us that the teacher should exhort pupils from the beginning to be very particular about their conduct:

"Let your conduct be marked by right action, including study and teaching of the scriptures; by truthfulness in word, deed, and thought, by self-denial and the practice of austerity; by poise and self-control; by performance of the every duties of life with a cheerful heart and an attached mind.

Speak the truth. Do your duty. Do not neglect the study of the scriptures. Do not cut thet hread of progeny. Swerve not from truth. Deviate not from the path of good. Rever greatness.

Let your mother be a god to you; let your father be a god to you. *Do only such actions as are blameless.*

Always show reverence to the great.

Whatever you give to others, give with love and reverence.

Gifts must be given in abundance, with joy, humility, and compassion.

If at any time there is any doubt with regard to right conduct, follow the practice of great souls, who are guideless, of good judgement, and devoted to truth.

Thus conduct yourself always. This is the injunction, this is the teaching, and this is the command of the scriptures."

(*Taittiriya* 1.xi)

It is the duty of every sensible being to preserve the glow of this inner truth that he is essentially the Infinite and therefore to wage wars and conflicts means denying one's own Infinite existence. He should resolve like Tagore:

"...I shall ever try to keep my body pure, knowing that Thy living touch is upon all my limbs. I shall ever try to keep all untruths out of my thoughts, knowing that Thou art that truth which has kindled the light of reason in my mind...And it shall be my endeavour to reveal Thee in my actions, knowing it is Thy strength that gives me strength to act." (*Gitanjali*, 4)

One should not think that the realization of becoming the Infinite is impossible. It is difficult to attain because of our ignorance of the Truth and unhelpful environment. But it is certainly attainable through sincere efforts. It is useful to remember the following words of Aldous Huxley in this context:

"Only the rather stupid and insentient, nowadays, have strong and sharply defined personalities. Only the barbarians among us 'know what they are'. The civilized are conscious of 'what they may be', and so are incapable of knowing what, for practical, social purposes, they actually are—have forgotten how to select a personality out of their total atomic experience".

(*Eyeless in Gaza*, p. 99)

Swami Vivekananda, the celebrated modern saint-philosopher has aptly pointed out:

"Just as unconscious plane is beneath consciousness, so there is another plane which is above consciousness, and which is not accompanied with the feeling of egoism. The feeling of egoism is only on the middle plane......By the effects, by the results of the work, we can know that which is below, and that which is above."[1]

Existentialism which tries to give importance to the individual in the West falls much short of the standard of truth because it equates 'I' only with the body. The word 'I' is treated as something devoid of its ontological purport.

For example according to Jean-Paul Sartre "There is nothing behind the body. But the body is wholly psychic."[2] Or let us take the following statement:

"I am body, for I am nothing apart from it, when I touch myself, I am thereby touched; when my body experiences pain or pleasure, it is I who experiences them" Gabriel Marcel also states that "...existential teaching about the body as an essential factor in existence directs men rather towards seeking to be at home in the body."[3]

Every one experiences the presence of the Infinite in some moments of his life. But every one does not persist in having a continuing experience of the type, because one's environment leads one to the ordinary world of finitude. That is why a systematic and concentrated effort is needed to have a constant vision of the Real. Humanity shall have to develop that capacity of the vision of the Infinite, if intends to get rid of the danger of universal destruction of mankind posed by the modern atomic weapons. If all the people cannot develop this capacity, at least some persons shall have to develop it to guide humanity in the right direction in this hour of universal gloom. There is no other way of escaping the universal disaster. Technological knowledge is sure to be used in a destructive manner unless the spirit of

1. The Complete Works of Swami Vivekananda-Mayavati, Almora, Advaita Ashram, 1931, p. 180.

2. Being and Nothingness: An Essay on Phenomenological Ontology, tr. Hazel Barnes, New York, 1956, p. 305.

3. Existentialism by John Macquarrie, Pelican Books, 1973, p. 70.

universal unity is developed. Man can develop this, as he has been able to develop his destructive potentiality. Man must be taught that he has great affinity to the spirit. In fact even the matter is an undeveloped spirit. The whole universe is nothing but the Infinite. If this capacity is not developed in near future, he shall have died and be born again to develop it. This process of death and birth shall continue till the perfect knowledge is gained and the Truth realized. Spiritual insight can save mankind from the tortures that await every period of darkness and death.

(C) SOUL-CENTERED RELIGION OF HUMANITY

Religion is one of the most important concepts of human culture. But it is difficult to get any uniform definition of religion. Even in the absence of any uniform concept of religion, one can be sure that religion is essentially an attempt to bind humanity, as it has been derived from the Latin term 'religare' meaning 'to bind'. That is why, even the *Chamber's Twentieth Century Dictionary* has described religion as "belief in, recognition of, or an awakened sense of, a higher unseen controlling power or powers, with the emotion and morality connected therewith."

Though the concept of religion is as old as the human being, there has been some evolution of the concept through the years. The primitive man believed in his primitive religion. But now we have reached the stage of the religion of humanity. Old gods have been discarded and humanity has taken their place. This change in the domain of religion is in keeping with the revolutionary changes that have taken place in the history of mankind.

It does not mean, however, that every human being has started believing in the religion of humanity. How can we forget that even individual minds have their stages of evolution ? Aurobindo has rightly observed: "The ghosts of things dead are very troublesome actualities and they now abound, ghosts of dead religions, dead arts, dead moralities, dead political theories, which still claim either to keep their rotting bodies or to animate partly the existing body of things. Repeating obstinately their sacred formulas of the past, they hypnotise backward-looking minds and daunt even the progressive portion of humanity."[1]

But the concept of the religion of humanity is slowly but steadily emerging.

It must, however, be accepted that the nature of this religion of humanity has not crystallised so far. To quote the words of Aurobindo "it may be either an intellectual and sentimental ideal, a living dogma with intellectual, psychological and practical effects, or else a spiritual aspiration and rule of living, and partly the sign, partly the cause of a change of soul in humanity."[2]

However, the process of evolution someday shall make the nature of this religion quite solid and objective.

The religion of humanity was put forth for the first time in the West in 18th century. Aurobindo calls it "the manasa putra of the rationalist thinkers who brought it forward as a substitute for the formal spiritualism of ecclesiastical Christianity." He proceeds to add "It tried to give itself a body in Positivism, which was an attempt to formulate the dogmas of this religion, but on too heavily and severely rationalistic a basis for acceptance even by an age of Reason."[3]

According to Aurobindo humanitarianism, philanthropy, social service etc. are merely the outward expression of this very religion of humanity. Not only this, even democracy, socialism, pacificim "are to a great extent its by-products or at least owe much of their vigour to its presence."[4]

Aurobindo has tried to define the nature of this religion of humanity in spiritual terms. "The fundamental idea is that mankind is the godhead to be worshipped and served by man." It follows from this that a follower of the religion of humanity must try to abandon the lesser gods like nationalism, the Church, the State or narrow-minded religion. It is not that these objects are totally rejected. What is done is that they are considered inferior to humanity, and if there is any conflict between humanity and these ideals, humanity-ideal must win.

1. Shri Aurobindo International Centre of Education Collection Vol. IX, Sri Aurobindo Ashram, Pondicherry, 1962, page 756.
2. *Ibid.*
3. *Ibid.*, p. 757.
4. *Ibid.*

Wellbeing of mankind is the sole objective to be ataitned. In the inimitable words of Aurobindo "No injunctions of old creeds, religious, political, social or cultural, are valid when they go against its claims."[1]

It should be noted that even Science, which occupies such an important position in the world, is considered valuable only so far as it serves humanity. If it goes against the interests of humanity, it must be rejected without any hesitation. This new religion abhors war, capital punishment, cruelty of all kinds, whether committed by the individual, the state or a community, the oppression and exploitation of man by man, of class by class, of nation by nation, in any garb, which have been sanctioned by old traditions and religions must be stopped, nay iradicated. This religion proclaims "Man must be sacred to man regardless of all distinctions of race, creed, colour, nationality, status, political or social advancement." Man has to be protected against disease, oppression, cruelty, penury and lack of security. "The life of man is to be held sacred, preserved, strengthened, ennobled, uplifted". This new religion demands that even the mind and the heart of man have to be protected from any kind of violence and given freedom to expand in right direction. Their development, however, should be directed that their powers are yoked for the service of humanity. As is clear, noble sentiments alone are not sufficient. They must be "given full and practical recognition in the persons of men and nations and mankind."

This is the idea and spirit of "the intellectual religion of humanity." This religion of humanity is surely a great advancement over the past religions which incited people to wage hundred years war and unleash a torrent of physical torture and violence on their so called opponents. Aurobindo has nothing but praise for this new religion. He gives his reasons for his appreciation.

"It accomplished rapidly many things which orthodox religion failed to do effectively, largely because it acted as a constant intellectual and critical solvent, an unsparing assailant of the thing that is an unflinching champion of the things to be,

1. *Ibid.*

faithful always to the future, while orthodox religion allied itself with the powers of the present, even of the past, bound itself by its pact with them and could act only at best as a moderating but not as a reforming force. Moreover, this religion has faith in humanity and its earthly future and can therefore aid its earthly progress, while the orthodox religions looked with eyes of pious sorrow and gloom on the earthly life of man and were very ready to bid him bear peacefully and contentedly, even to welcome its crudities, cruelties, oppressions, tribulations as a means for learning to appreciate and for earning the better life which will be given us hereafter."[1]

Aurobindo is full of praise for this religion of humanity. This religion has great utility. It has 'humanised society, humanised law and punishment, humanised the outlook of man on man, abolished legalised torture and the cruder forms of slavery, raised those who were depressed and fallen, gave large hopes to humanity, stimulated philanthropy and charity and the service of mankind, encouraged everywhere the desire of freedom, put a curh on oppression and greatly minimised its more brutal expressions.'

Not only this, according to Aurobindo it had already succeeded in 'humanising war and would perhaps have succeeded entirely but for the contrary trend of modern Science.' Thanks to this religion, for it has made it possible for man to conceive of a world free from war as imaginable 'even without waiting for the Christian millennium.' We should not forget that prior to the dawn of this new religion 'peace was a rare interlude of constant war.' But due to the influence of this new religion of humanity war has become an interlude.

Now the world has new conceptions of the dignity of the human being. Man, for the first time in human history has been given some importance. That is why the distinctions of the serf and the master, owner and the labourer, the rich and the poor are thinning down. We have new ideas about education and development of human personality. Our old ideals of supermen trodding their fellow-beings have been thrown out. Now we think about striking out the distinctions between man and man.

1. *Ibid.*, p. 759.

Democracy, Communism and such other social and political ideals have been accepted throughout the world. To talk about imperialism and dictatorship is to lower ourselves in these days. People at least a great majority of them decry ideas. In one word, we can say that the new religion has brought enlightenment to our mankind.

Thus the accomplishment of the religion of humanity is obvious. Yet it has yet to accomplish much. The human beings have not been given their proper importance even now, though an attempt in that direction has been made. There is only a beginning. The ultimate objective has not been attained as yet. The world has to move much further. That means that the religion of humanity 'has to make itself more explicit, insistent and categorically imperative'. This religion must become not only more popular, it must also be stronger. At present merely a small number of people can understand this religion. That is why its strength is limited.

We must understand this fact that its chief enemy is human egoism. According to Aurobindo 'the enemy of all real religion, is human egoism, the egoism of the individual, the egoism of class and nation.'[1] Unless this egoism is mastered, no progress is possible.

This egoism is so strong that it cannot be eliminated easily. However, it can be softened for some time. And it must be recognised that the religion of humanity cannot rest content till it achieves its final objective viz. a living sense of human oneness and practice of human oneness in thought, feeling and life.

According to Aurobindo, this final aim of the religion of humanity has drawn inspiration from the Vedic injunction of human unity. In fact basic teaching of the Indian philosophy is to underline the unity of mankind. The Bhagavadgita states emphatically that the Lord is present in everything. Even the lowly and undeveloped beings are not devoid of the presence of this Lord.[2]

Aurobindo points out that till this unity is brought about in

1. *Ibid.*, p. 761.
2. *The Bhagvadagita*, VI-30, VII 7.

the minds of people 'the religion of humanity remains unaccomplished.' This 'psychological change' is not only essential, but even desirable, because the ultimate objective of religion of humanity cannot be attained by "catastrophic means". The outward, formal and mechanical political changes are incapable of leading humanity to its aim. Real progress in the world can come only when we have 'perfected and developed' human nature."

Aurobindo is of the opinion that our present religion of humanity, which is 'a purely intellectual and sentimental religion,' cannot deliver the goods. He affirms: "The intellect and the feelings are merely instruments of the being and they may be the instruments of either its lower external form or of the inner and higher man, servants of the ego or channels of the soul." It is clear from the fact that although historically the aim of the religion of humanity was conceived in terms of liberty, equality and fraternity as early as 18th century, none of these ideals have been attained even by this time. The liberty has been confused with 'an outward and mechanical and unreal liberty'; the equality has been made an outward and mechanical' thing and is far from real equality; and fraternity has been misconceived as the outward and mechanical principle of equal association or at the best a comradeship of labour."

Why has this deterioration taken place? Aurobindo's answer is: "This is because the idea of humanity has been obliged in an intellectual age to mask its true character of a religion and a thing of the soul and the spirit and to appeal to the vital and physical mind of man rather than his inner being. It has limited his effort to the attempt to revolutionise political and social institutions and to bring about such a modification of the ideas and sentiments of the common mind of mankind as would make these institutions practicable; it has worked at the machinery of human life and on the outer mind much more than upon the soul of the race."[1]

Aurbindo is of the opinion that the political, legal and social revolutions that are aims of the religion of humanity cannot be achieved unless they are based on 'a change of the inner human

1. Vol. IX, p. 763.

nature and inner way of living.' If we desire to achieve the higher ideals of freedom, equality and brotherhood, we must destroy 'the individual and the communal ego.' Unless this ego is destroyed, the equality that we shall get shall be artificial, the liberty shall be a mere competitive individualism, for 'the ego to speak of fraternity is for it to speak of something contrary to its nature.' The common egoistic ends can give us exploitation in some new and more dangerous form.

Brotherhood is the key principle which can give us a world untouched by exploitation of any kind. But this brotherhood can exist only in the soul. 'It can exist by nothing else.' The three principles of freedom, equality and unity are really speaking 'the eternal attributes of the Spirit.'[1]

We can therefore conclude that real religion of humanity can flourish only when it starts believing in soul and spirit. If spirit is denied, the denial of equality, liberty and fraternity too follows. Spiritual religion alone can help us in attaining our social objectives.

Aurobindo is quite right. Denial of spirit has reduced communism to some kind of dictatorship, and it has reduced democracy to a rule of opportunists. Humanity has gained nothing substantially. We must try to found our religion of humanity on the soul to get proper results.

1. *Ibid*, p. 764.

CHAPTER 3

SIGNIFICANT SELECTION OF UTTERANCES: FROM LORD SHRIKRISHNA TO EX-PRIME MINISTER MORARJI DESAI

1. THE MAHABHARATA

THE MAHABHARATA is the most important epic of India. It is not only an epic; it is a history of a great battle fought between the sons of Dhritarashtra and the sons of Pandu.

Sometimes it is stated that the Mahabharata is not a history, but an allegory representing an inner conflict between the good and evil tendencies of a person. The allegory can be interpreted even otherwise. It is a story of war-mongers, exploiters and immoral leaders of human society on one hand, and their conflict with the peace-lovers moral-minded people on the other hand. The Kauravas led by Duryodhana represent the former, while Pandawas led by Shrikrishna represent latter. If interpreted in this way, the Mahabharata appears as a great work of perennial significance. It tries to impress on the minds of its readers that victory waits on righteousness (yato dharmas tato jayah).

Radhakrishna has rightly stated: "Though the Mahabharata

describes a society distracted by deceit and intrigue and though the story is reeking with war and the spirit of war, the author clearly declares himself against the politics of power and looks upon the state not as an organisation of force but as a partnership in dharma."

The Mahabharata is a receptacle of ageless truths. That is why it is still relevant to our modern society which is facing its extinction due to the invention of atomic weapons and neutron bombs. In the selection being included in the present volume, Shrikrishna tries to plead for peace with Duryodhana. We have to replace any warring nation or its head instead of Duryodhana and any nation or its head whose just rights are ignored by a powerful nation. Shrikrishna's speech then shall be understood properly and his attempt for peace shall be duly realised.

Shrikrishna clearly declares to Vidura who knew that Duryodhana would never accept peace and therefore former's peace effort was futile "Great will be the merit earned by him who will liberate from the meshes of death the whole earth, with her elephants, cars, and steads, overwhelmed with a dreadful calamity. If a man striving to the best of his abilities to perform a virtuous act meets with failure, I have not the least doubt that the merit of that act becomes his, notwithstanding such failure."

Yudhisthira, the eldest of the Pandawas too tells Shrikrishna: "Both parties cannot win success, nor both be defeated. The loss, however, on both sides may be equal. If one flieth away, loss of both life and expense is his. Under all circumstances, however, war is a sin. Who in striking another is not struck himself ? As regards the person, however, who is struck, victory and defeat, Hrishikesha, are the same. It is true that defeat is not much removed from death, but his loss also, O Krishna, is not less who winneth victory. He himself may not be killed, but his adversaries will kill at least some one that is dear to him, or some others, and thus the man, O Sire, deprived of strength and not seeing before him his sons and brothers, becometh indifferent, O Krishna, to life itself. Those that are quiet, modest, virtuous, and compassionate, are generally slain in battle, while they that are wicked escape. Even after slaying one's foes, repentance, O Janardana, possesseth the heart! He that surviveth among the foes giveth trouble, for the survivor, collecting a force, seeketh to destroy the surviving victors.

Even Bhima says: "All of us, O Krishna, would rather in humiliation follow Duryodhana submissively, but, oh, let not the Bharatas be annihilated."

The Mahabharata is a work that emphasises the desirability of peace points out the destruction that wars causes. That is why it has a pointed value even for our age.

A. KRISHNA'S SPEECH RECOMMENDING PEACE

Vaishampayana said.—"And after all the kings had been seated and a perfect silence had ensued, Krishna possessing fine teeth and having a voice deep as that of the drum, begain to speak. And Madhava, although he addressed Dhritarashtra, spoke in a voice deep as the roll of clouds in the rainy season, making the whole assembly hear. And he said,—"In order that, O Bharata, peace may be established between the Kurus and the Pandavas without a slaughter of heroes, I have come hither! Besides this, O king, I have no other beneficial words to utter. O chastiser of foes, everything that should be learned in this world is already known to thee! This thy race, O king, owing to its learning and behaviour, and owing also to its being adorned with every accomplishment, is most distinguished among all royal dynasties. Joy in the happiness of others, grief at sight of other people's misery, desire to alleviate distress, abstention from injury, sincerity, forgiveness, and truth,—these, O Bharata, prevail amongst the Kurus! Whey thy race, therefore, O king, is so noble it would be a pity if anything improper were done by any one belonging to it, and a greater pity still if it were done by thee! O chief of the Kurus, thou art the first of those that should restrain the Kurus, if they behave deceitfully towards strangers or those numbering with themselves: Know, O thou of Kuru's race, that those wicked sons of thine headed by Duryodhana, abandoning both virtue and profit, disregarding morality, and deprived of their senses of avarice, are now acting most unrighteously towards, O bull of men, their foremost of kinsmen! That terrible danger which threatens all, hath its origin in the conduct of the Kurus! If thou becomest indifferent to it, will then produce a universal slaughter! If, O Bharata, thou art willing, thou mayst be able to allay that danger even yet, for, O bull of Bharata's race, peace, I think, is not difficult of acquisition! The establishment of peace, O king, depends on thee and myself, O monarch! Set right thy sons, O thou of Kuru's race, and I will set the Pandavas right!, Whatever be thy command, O king, it behoveth thy sons with their followers to obey it! If again they live in obedience to thee, that would be the very best they could do. If thou strivest for peace by restraining the sons, it will be to thy profit, O king, as also to the profit of the Pandavas! Having reflected carefully, act thou thyself, O king! Let those sons of Bharata (the Pandavas) be, O ruler of men, they allies! Supported by the Pandavas, O king, seek thou both religion and profit! By every exertion in thy power thou canst not have, O king, such allies as they who are such! Protected by the illustrious sons of Pandu, Indra himself at the head of the celestials will not be able to vanquish thee! How would it be possible then for mere earthly kings to bear thy prowess? There where Bhishma, and Drona, and Kripa, and Karna, and Vivingshati, and Ashwathaman, and Vikarna, and Somadatta, and Vahlika, and the chief of the Sindhus, and the ruler of the Kalingas, and Sudakshina the king of the Kamvojas, and Yudhishthira, and Bhimasena, and Savyasachin, and the twins, and Satyaki of mighty energy, and Yuyutsu that mighty car-warrior, are stationed, who is there, O bull of Bharata's race, of such misdirected intelligence that would fight these? If, O slayer of foes, thou hast both the Kurus and the Pandavas at thy back, the sovereignty of the whole world and invincibility before all foes will be thine! All rulers of the earth, O monarch, that are either equal to thee or superior, will then seek alliance with thee! Protected on all sides by sons, grandsons, fathers, brothers and friends, thou will then be able to live in exceeding happiness! Keeping these before thee and treating them with kindness as in days of yore, thou, O monarch, wilt enjoy the sovereignty of the whole earth! With these as thy supporters and with the sons of Pandu also, thou wilt, O Bharata, be able to conquer all thy foes!, Even this is thy best advantage. If, O chastiser of foes, thou art united with thy sons and kinsmen and counsellors, thou wilt enjoy the sovereignty of the whole earth won for thee by them! In battle, O great king, nothing but wholesale destruction is visible. Indeed, in the destruction of both parties what merit dost thou see? If the Pandawas are slaughtered in battle, or if thy own mighty sons fall, tell me, O bull of Bharata's race, what happiness wilt thou enjoy? All of them are brave and skilled in weapons. All of them are desirous of battle, the Pandaws as also thy sons. Oh, save them from the terrible danger that threatens them. After the battle thou wilt not behold all the Kurus or all the Pandawas. Car warriors slain by car-warriors, thou wilt behold the heroes of both parties reduced in numbers and strength. All the rulers of the earth, O best of kings, have been assembled together. Inflamed with wrath, they will certainly exterminate the population of the earth. Save O king, the world. Let not the population of the earth be exterminated. O son of Kuru's race, if thou regainest the natural disposition, the earth may continue to be peopled as now. Save, O king, these monarchs who are all of pure descent, endued with modesty and liberality and piety, and connected with one another in bonds of relationship or alliance, from the terrible danger that threatens them. Abandoning wrath and enmity, O chastiser of foes, let these kings, embracing one another in peace, eating and drinking with one another, dressed in excellent robes and decked with garlands, and doing courtesies to one another, return to their respective homes. Let the affection thou hadst for the Pandawas be revived in thy bosom, and let it, O bull of Bharata's race, lead to the establishment of peace. Deprived of their father while they were infants, they were brought up by thee. Cherish them now as becomes thee, O bull of Bharata's race, as if they were thy own sons. It is thy duty to protect them. And especially is it so when they are distressed. O bull of Bharata's race, let not thy virtue and profit be both lost. Saluting and propitiating thee, the Pandawas have said unto thee—At thy command we have, with our followers, suffered great misery. For these twelve years have we lived in the woods, and for the thirteenth year have we lived *incognito* in an inhabited part of the world. We broke not our pledge, firmly believing that our father would also be abide by his. That we violated not our word is well-known to the Brahmanas who were with us. And as we, O bull of the Bharata's race, have abided by our promise, also do thou abide by thine. Long have we suffered the great misery, but let us now have our share of the kingdom. Fully conversant as thou art with virtue and profit, it behoveth thee to rescue us. Knowing that our obedience is due to thee, we have quietly undergone much misery. Behave thou then unto us like a father or brother. A preceptor should behave as a preceptor towards his disciples, and as disciples we are willing to behave as such towards thee our preceptor! Act thou, therefore, towards us as a preceptor should. If we go wrong, it is the duty of our father to set us right. Therefore, set us on the way, and trend thou also the excellent path of righteousness! Those sons of thine, O bull of the Bharata's race, have also said unto these kings assembled in thy court these words:—If the members of an assembly are conversant with morality, nothing improper should be permitted by them to happen. Where, in the presence of the virtuous members of an assembly, righteousness is sought to be overpowered by unrighteousness and truth by the untruth, it is those members themselves that are vanquished and slain. When righteousness, pierced by unrighteousness, seeketh the protection of an assembly, if the arrow is not extracted, it is the members themselves that are pierced by that arrow. Indeed, in that case, righteousness slayeth the members of that assembly like a river eating away the roots of the trees on its bank!—Judge now, O bull of the the Bharata's race! The Pandavas, with their eyes turned towards righteousness and reflecting on everything, are maintaining a calm attitude and what they have said is consistent with truth and virtue and justice. O ruler of men, what canst thou say unto them but that thou art willing to give them back their kingdom?, Let these rulers of earth that are sitting here say (what the answer should be)! If it appears to thee that what I have said after reflecting well on virtue to be true, save them, O bull of the Bharata race, all the Kshatriyas from the meshes of death! Affect peace, O chief of Bharata's race, and yield not to anger! Giving unto the Pandavas their just share of the paternal kingdom, enjoy thou then, with thy sons, O chastiser of foes, happiness and luxury, thy wishes being all crowned with success! Know that Yudhishthira always treadeth path that is trod by the righteous. Thou knowest also, O king, what the behaviour of Yudhishthira is towards thee and thy sons! Although thou hadst sought to burn him to death and hadst exiled him from human habitation, yet he came back and once more reposed confidence in thee! Again didst thou, with thy sons, banish him to Indraprastha! While living there, he brought all the kings of the earth to subjection and yet looked to thy face, O king, without seeking to disregard thee! Although he behaved in this way, yet Suvala's son, desirous of robbing him of his dominions and wealth and possessions, applied the very efficacious means of dice! Reduced to that condition and even beholding Krishna dragged into the assembly, Yudhishthira of immeasurable soul did not yet swerve from the duties of a Kshatriya! As regards myself, I desire, O Bharata, thy good as also theirs! For the sake of virtue, of profit, of happiness, make peace, O king, and do not allow the Earth's population to be slaughtered, regarding evil as good and good as evil! Restrain thy sons, O monarch, who have from convetousness proceeded too far! As regards the sons of Pritha, they are equally ready to wait upon thee in dutiful service as to fight! That which, O chastiser of foes, seems to thee to be for thy good, do thou adopt!"

B. YOGI AUROBINDO

Yogi Aurobindo was a great political fighter, philosopher and mystic. Romain Rolland regarded him as the highest synthesis of the genius of Europe and the genius of Asia. Rabindranath Tagore hailed him as a great exponent of the spiritual message of India and Radhakrishnan declared him to be the greatest intellectual of our age.

He was a great exponent of the ideal of human unity, because he considered man essentially spiritual in content. He spoke about it in his one of the poems:

Therefore must Time
Still batter down the glory and form of youth
And animal magnificent strong ease,
To warn the earthward man that he is spirit
Dallying with transcience, nor by death he ends,
Not to be dumb warm mother's arms is bound
But called unborn into the unborn skies.

INTERNATIONALISM

The idea of humanity as a single race of beings with a common life and a common general interest is among the most characteristic and significant products of modern thought. It is an outcome of the European mind which proceeds characteristically from life-experience to the idea and, without going deeper, returns from the idea upon life in an attempt to change its outward forms and institutions, its order and system. In the European mentality it has taken the shape known currently as internationalism. Internationalism is the attempt of the human mind and life to grow out of the national idea and form and even in a way to destroy it in the interest of the larger synthesis of mankind. An idea proceeding on these lines needs always to attach itself to some actual force or developing power in the life of the times before it can exercise a practical effect. But usually it suffers by contact with the interest and prepossessions of its grosser ally some lesser or greater diminution of itself or even a distortion, and in that form, no longer pure and absolute, enters on the first stage of practice.

The idea of internationalism was born of the thought of the eighteenth century and it took some kind of voice in the idealistic stages of the French Revolution. But at that time, it was rather a vague intellectual sentiment than a clear idea seeing its way to practice; it found no strong force in life to help it to take visible body. What came out of the French Revolution and the struggle that grew around it, was a complete and self-conscious nationalism and not internationalism. During the nineteeth century we see the larger idea growing again in the minds of thinkers, sometimes in a modified form, sometimes in its own pure idealism, till allying itself with the growing forces of socialism and anarchism it took a clear body and a recognisable vital force. In its absolute form, it became the internationalism of the intellectuals, intolerant of nationalism as a narrow spirit of the past, contemptuous of patriotism as an irrational prejudice, a maleficent corporate egoism characteristic of narrow intellects and creative of arrogance, prejudice, hatred, oppression, division and strife between nation and nation, a gross survival of the past which the growth of reason was destined to destroy. It is founded on a view of things which looks at man in his manhood only and casts away all those physical and social accidents of birth, rank, class, colour, creed, nationality, which have been erected into so many walls and screens behind which man has hidden himself from his fellow-man; he has turned them into sympathy-proof shelters and trenches from which he wages against him a war of defence and aggression, war of nations, war of continents, war of classes, war of colour with colour, creed with creed, culture with culture. All this barbarism the idea of the intellectual internationalist seeks to abolish by putting man face to face with man on the basis of their common human sympathy, aims, highest interests of the future. It is entirely futurist in its view; it turns away from the confused and darkened good of the past to the purer good of the future when man, at last beginning to become a truly intelligent and ethical being will shake away from him all these sources of prejudice and passion and evil. Humanity will become one in idea and feeling, and life be consciously what it now is in spite of itself, one in its status on earth and its destiny.

The height and nobility of the idea is not to be questioned and certainly a mankind which set its life upon this basis would make a better, purer, more peaceful and enlightened race than anything we can hope to have at present. But as the human being is now made, the pure idea, though always a great power, is also afflicted by a great weakness. It has an eventual capacity, once born, of taking hold of the rest of the human being and forcing him in the end to acknowledge its truth and make some kind of attempt to embody it; that is its strength. But also because man at present lives more in the outward than in the inward, is governed principally by his vital existence, sensations, feelings and customary mentality rather than by his higher thought mind, and feels himself in these to be really alive, really to exist and be while the world of ideas is to him something remote and abstract and, however, powerful and interesting in its way, not a living thing, the pure idea seems, until it is embodied in life, something not quite real; in that abstractness and remoteness lies its weakness.

The sense of this abstractness imposes on the idea an undue haste to get itself recognised by life and embodied in a form. If it could have confidence in its strength and be content to grow, to insist, to impress itself till it got well into the spirit of man, it might conceivably become a real part of his soul-life, a permanent power in his psychology and might succeed in remoulding his whole life in its image. But it has inevitably a desire to get as soon as possible admitted into a form of the life, for until then it does not feel itself strong and cannot quite be sure that it has vindicated its truth. It hurries into action before it has real knowledge of itself and thereby prepares its own disappointment, even when it seems to triumph and fulfil its object. For in order to succeed, it allies itself with powers and movements which are impelled by another aim than its own, but are glad enough to get its aid so that they may strengthen their own case and claim. Thus when it realises itself at last, it does it in a mixed, impure and ineffective form. Life accepts it as a partial habit, but not completely, not quite sincerely. That has been the history of every idea in succession and one reason at least why there is almost always something unreal, inconclusive and tormented about human progress.

There are many conditions and tendencies in human life at present which are faviourable to the progress of the internationalist idea. The strongest of these favourable forces is the constant drawing closer of the knots of international life, the multiplication of points of contact and threads of communication and an increasing community in thought, in Science and in knowledge. Science especially has been a great force in this direction for Science is a thing common to all men in its conclusions, open to all in its methods, available to all in its results: it is international in its very nature; there can be no such thing as a national Science, but only the nations' contributions to the work and growth of Science which are the indivisible inheritance of all humanity. Therefore, it is easier for men of Science or those strongly influenced by Science to grow into the international spirit and all the world is now beginning to feel the scientific influence and to live in it. Science also has created that closer contact of every part of the world with every other part, out of which some sort of international mind is growing. Even cosmopolitian habits of life are now not uncommon and there are a fair number of persons who are as much or more citizens of the world as citizens of their own nation. The growth of knowledge is interesting the peoples in each other's art, culture, religion, ideas and is breaking down at many points the prejudice, arrogance and exclusiveness of the old nationalistic sentiment. Religion, which ought to have led the way, but owing to its greater dependence on its external parts and its infrarational rather than its spiritual impulses, has been as much, or even more, a sower of discord as a teacher of unity,—religion is beginning to realise, a little dimly and ineffectively as yet, that spirituality is after all its own chief business and true aim and that it is also the common element and the common bond of all religions. As these influences grow and come more and more consciously to co-operate with each other, it might be hoped that the necessary psychological modification will quietly, gradually, but still irresistibly and at least with an increasing force of rapidity, take place which can prepare a real fundamental change in the life of humanity.

But this is at present a slow process, and meanwhile the internationalist idea, eager for effectuation, allied and almost identified itself with two increasingly powerful movements which have both assumed an international character, Socialism and Anarchism. Indeed, it is this alliance that most commonly went by the name of internationalism. But this socialistic and anarchistic internationalism was recently put to the test, the fiery test of the European war, and thus tried, it was found sadly wanting. In every country, the Socialist party shed its internationalist promise with the greatest ease and lightness, German socialism, the protagonist of the idea, massively leading the way in this formidable abjuration. It is true that a small minority in each country either remained heroically faithful to its principles or soon returned to them, and as the general weariness of the great international massacre grew, even the majority showed a sensible turn in the same direction; but this was rather the fruit of circumstance than of principle. Russian socialism, it may be said, has, at least in its extremer form, shown a stronger root of internationalistic feeling. But what it has actually attempted to accomplish is a development of labour rule on the basis of a purified nationalism, non-aggrsseive except for revolutionary purposes and self-contained, and not on the larger international idea. In any case, the actual results of the Russian attempt show only up to the present a failure of the idea to acquire the vital strength and efficiency which would justify it to life; it is possible to use them much more as a telling argument against internationalism than as a justification of its truth or at least of its applicability in the present stage of human progress.

But what is the cause of this almost total bankruptcy of the international idea under the strong test of life ? Partly it may be because the triumph of socialism is not necessarily bound up with the progress of internationalism. Socialism is really an attempt to complete the growth of the national community by making the Individual do what he has never yet done, live for the community more than for himself. It is an outgrowth of the national, not of the international idea. No doubt, when the society of the nation has been perfected, the society of nations can and even must be formed; but this is a later possible or eventual result of Socialism, not its primary vital necessity. In the crises of life it is the primary vital necessity which tells, while the other and remoter element betrays itself to be a mere idea not yet ready for accomplishment; it can only become powerful when it also becomes either a vital or a psychological necessity. The real truth, the real cause of the failure is that internationalism is as yet, except with some exceptional men, merely an idea; it is not yet a thing near to our vital feelings or otherwise a part of our psychology. The normal socialist or syndicalist cannot escape from the general human feeling and in the test he too turns out, even though he were a professed snas-patrie in ordinary times, in his inner heart and being a nationalist. As a vital fact, moreover, these movements have been a revolt of Labour aided by a number of intellectuals against the established state of things, and they have only allied themselves with internationalism, because that too is an intellectual revolt and because its idea helps them in the battle. If Labour comes to power, will it keep or shed its internationalistic tendencies ? The experience of countries in which it is or has been at the head of affairs does not give an encouraging answer, and it may at least be said that, unless at that time the psychological change in humanity has gone much further than it has now, Labour in power is likely to shed more of the internationalist feeling than it will succeed in keeping and to act very much from the old human motives

No doubt, the European war itself was an explosion of all that was dangerous and evil in successful nationalism, and the resulting conflagration may well turn out to have been a purificatory process that has burned up many things that needed to die. It has already strengthened the international idea and forced it on governments and peoples. But we cannot rely too greatly on ideas and resolutions formed in a moment of abnormal crises under the violent stress of exceptional circumstances. Some effect there may be in the end, some first recognition of juster principles in international dealings, some attempt at a better, more rational or at least a more convenient international order. But until the idea of humanity has grown not only upon the intelligence but in the sentiments, feelings, natural sympathies and mental habits of men, the progress made is likely to be more in external adjustments than in the vital matters, more in a use of the ideal for mixed and egoistic purposes than at once or soon in a large and sincere realization of the ideal. Until man in his heart is ready, a profound change of the world conditions cannot come; or it can only be brought about by force, physical force or else force of circumstances, and that leaves all the real work to be done. A frame may have then been made, but the soul will have still to grow into that mechanical body.

INTERNATIONALISM AND HUMAN UNITY

The great necessity, then, and the great difficulty is to help this idea of humanity which is already at work upon our minds and has even begun in a very slight degree to influence from above our actions, and turn it into something more than an idea, however strong, to make it a central motive and a fixed part of our nature. Its satisfaction must become a necessity of our psychological being, just as the family idea or the national idea has become each a psychological motives with its own need of satisfaction. But how is this to be done ? The family idea had the advantage of growing out of a primary vital need in our being and therefore it had not the least difficulty in becoming a psychological motive and need; are for our readiest and strongest mental motives and psychological needs are those which grow out of our vital necessities and instincts. The clan and the tribe ideas had a similar origin, less primary and compelling, and therefore looser and more dissoluble; but still they arose from the vital necessity in human nature for aggregation and the ready basis given to it by the inevitable physical growth of the family into clan or tribe. These were natural aggregations, evolutionary forms already prepared on the animal level.

The nation idea, on the contrary, did not arise from a primary vital need, but from a secondary or even tertiary necessity which resulted not from anything inherent in our vital nature, but from circumstances, from environmental evolution: it arose not from a vital, but from a geographical and historical necessity. And we notice that as one result it had to be created most commonly by force, force of circumstance partly, no doubt, but also by physical force, by the power of the king and the conquering tribe converted into a military and dominant State. Or else it came by a reaction against force, a revolt against conquest and domination that brought a slow or sudden compactness to peoples who, though geographically or even historically and culturally one, had lacked power of cohesion and remained too conscious of an original heterogeneity or of local and regional and other divisions. But still the necessity was there, and the nation form after many failures and false successes got into being, and the psychological motive of patriotism, a sign of the growth of a conscious national ego, arose in the form as the expression of its soul and the guarantee of its durability. For without such a soul, such a psychological force and presence within the frame there can be no guarantee of durability. Without it, what circumstances have created, circumstances easily will destroy. It was for this reason that the ancient world failed to create nations, except on a small scale, little clans and small regional nations of brief duration and usually of loose structure; it created only artificial empires which went to pieces and left chaos behind them.

What then of this international unity now in the first obscure throes of the preformatory state resembling a ferment of cells drawing together for amalgamation? What is the compelling necessity behind it? If we look at outward things only, the necessity is much less direct and much less compelling than any that preceded it. There is here no vital necessity; mankind as a whole can get on well enough without international unity, so far as mere living goes; it will not be at all a perfect, rational or ideal collective living of the race,-but after all where is there yet any element in human life or society which is perfect, rational or ideal? As yet at least none; still we get on somehow with life, because the vital man in us, who is the dominant element in our instincts and in our actions, cares for none of these things and is quite satisfied with any just tolerable or any precariously or partly agreeable form of living, because that is all to which he is accustomed and all therefore that he feels to be necessary. The men who are not satisfied, the thinkers, the idealists, are always a minority and in the end an ineffectual minority, because though always in the end they do get their way partly, their victory yet turns into a defeat; for the vital man remains still the majority and degrades the apparent success into a pitiful parody of their rational hope, their clear-sighted ideal or their strong counsel of perfection.

The geographical necessity for a unification of this kind does not exist, unless we consider that it has been created through the drawing closer together of the earth and its inhabitants by Science and her magical lessening of physical distances and attenuation of barriers. But whatever may happen in the future, this is an yet not sufficient, earth is still large enough and her divisions still real enough for her to do without any formal unity. If there is any strong need, it may be described—if such an epithet can be applied to a thing in the present and the future —as a historical necessity, that is, a need which has arisen as the result of certain ctual acircumstances that have grown up in the evolution of international relations. And that need is economic, political, mechanical, likely under certain circumstances to create some tentative or preliminary framework, but not at first a psychological reality which will vivify the frame. Moreover, it is not yet sufficiently vital to be precisely a necessity; for it amounts mainly to a need for the removal of certain perils and inconveniences, such as the constant danger of war, and at most to the strong desirability of a better international co-ordination. But by itself this creates only a possibility, not even a moral certainty, of a first vague sketch and loose framework of unity which may or may not lead to something more close and real.

But there is another power than that of external circumstance which we have a right to take into consideration. For behind all the external circumstances and necessities of which we are more easily aware in Nature, there is always an internal necessity in the being, a will and a design in Nature itself which precedes the outward singles of its development and in spite of all obstacles and failures must in the long end inevitably get itself realised. Nowadays we can see this truth everywhere in Nature down to her lowest forms; a will in the very seed of the being, not quite conscious or only partially conscious in the form itself, but still present there in Nature. It is subconscious or even inconscient if you like, but it is still a blind will, a mute idea which contains beforehand the form it is going to create, is aware of a necessity other than the environmental, a necessity contrained in the very being itself, and creates persistently and inevitably a form that best answers to the necessity, however we may labour to interfere with or thwart its operations.

This is true biologically, but it is also, though in a more subtle and variable way, psychologically true. Now the very nature of man is that of a individual who on one side is always emphasising and developing his individual being to the extent of his power but who is also driven by the Idea or Truth within him to unify himself with others of his species, to join himself to them or agglutinate them to him, to create human groups, aggregates and collectivities. And if there is an aggregate or collectivity which it is possible for him to realise but is not yet realised, we may be sure that that too in the end he will create. This will in him is not always or often quite conscient or foreseeing; it is often largely subconscient but even then it is eventually irresistible. And if it gets into his conscious mind, as the international idea has now done, we may count on a more rapid evolution. Such a will in Nature creates for itself favourable external circumstances and happenings or finds them created for it in the stress of events. And even if they are insufficient, she will still often use them beyond their apparent power of effectivity, not minding the possibility of failure, for she knows that in the end she will succeed and every experience of failure will help to better the eventual success.

Well then, it may be said, let us trust to this inevitable will in Nature and let us follow out her method of operation. Let us create anyhow this framework, any framework of the aggregate; for she knows already the complete form she intends and she will work out eventually in her own time by the power of the idea and our will to realise it, by help of strong force of circumstances, by pressure of all kinds, by physical force even, if need be, since that too seems still to be a part of her necessary machinery; let us create it. Let us have the body; the soul will grow in the body. And we need not mind if the bodily formation is artificial with at first a small or no conscious psychological reality to vivify it. That will begin to form itself as soon as the body has been formed; for the nation too was at first more or less artificially formed out of incoherent elements actually brought together by the necessity of a subconscient idea, though apparently it was done only by physical force and the force of circumstances. As a national ego formed which identified itself with the geographical body of the nation and developed in it the psychological instinct of national unity and the need of its satisfaction, so a collective human ego will develop in the international body and will evolve in it the psychological instinct of human unity and the need of its satisfaction. That will be guarantee of duration. And that possibly is how the thing will happen, man being what he is; indeed if we cannot do better, it will so happen, since happen somehow it must, whether in the worse way or the better.

It may be as well to review here briefly in the light of these considerations the main possibilities and powers which are shaping us towards such an end in the present world conditions. The old means of unification, conquest by a single great Power, which would reduce part of the world by force and bring the remaining nations into the condition of dependencies, protectorates and dependent allies, the whole forming the basic structure of a great final unification,--this was the character of the ancient Roman precedent,—does not seem immediately possible. It would require a great predominance of force simultaneously by sea and land, an irresistibly superior science and organisation and with all this a constantly successful diplomacy and an invincible good fortune. If war and diplomacy are still to be the decisive factors in international politics in the future as in the past, it would be rash to predict that such a combination may not arise, and if other means fail, it must arise; for there is nothing that can be set down as impossible in the chances of the future, and the urge in Nature always creates its own means. But, at present, the possibilities of the future do not seem to point in this direction. There is no, on the other hand, a very strong possibility of the whole earth, or at least the three continents of the eastern hemisphere, being dominated by three or four great empires largely increased in extent of dominion, spheres of influence, protectorates, and thereby exercising a pre-eminence which they could either maintain by agreements, avoiding all causes of conflict, or in a rivalry which would be the cause of fresh wars and changes. This would normally have been the result of the great European conflict.

But there has struck across this possibility a revived strength of the idea of nationality expressed in the novel formula of the principle of self-determination to which the great world-empires have had to pay at least a verbal homage. The idea of international unity to which this intervention of the revived force of nationality is leading, takes the form of a so-called League of Nations. Practically, however, the League of Nations under present conditions or any likely to be immediately realised would still mean the control of the earth by a few great Powers, —a control that would be checked only by the necessity of conciliating the sympathy and support of the more numerous smaller or less powerful nations. On the force and influence of these few would rest practically, if not admittedly, the decision of all important debatable questions. And without it there could be no chance of enforcing the decisions of the majority against any recalcitrant great Power or combination of Powers. The growth of democratic institutions would perhaps help to minimise the chances of conflict and of the abuse of power,— though that is not at all certain; but it would not alter this real character of the combination.

In all this there is no immediate prospect of any such form of unification as would give room for a real psychological sense of unity, much less necessitate its growth. Such a form might evolve; but we should have to trust for it to the chapter of accidents or at best to the already declared urge in Nature expressed in the internationalist idea. On that side, there was at one time a possibility which seemed to be very suddenly and rapidly growing into something more, the emergence of a powerful party in all the advanced countries of the world pledged to internationalism, conscious of its necessity as a first condition for their other aims and more and more determined to give it precedence and to unite internationally to bring it about. That combination of the intellectuals with Labour which created the Socialist parties in Germany, Russia and Austria, formed anew recently the Labour party in England and has had its counterparts in most other European countries, seems to be travelling in that direction. This world-wide movement which made internationalism and Labour rule its two main principles, had already created the Russian revolution and seemed ready to bring about another great socialistic revolution in central Europe. It was conceivable that this party might everywhere draw together. By a chain of revolutions such as took place in the nineteenth century and of less violent but still rapid evolutions brought about by the pressure of their example, or even by simply growing into the majority in each country, the party might control Europe. It might create counterparts of itself in all the American republics and in Asiatic countries. It might by using the machinery of the League of Nations or, where necessary, by physical force or economic or other pressure persuade or compel all the nations into some more stringent system of international unification. A World-State or else a close confederation of democratic peoples might be created with a common governing body for the decision of principles and for all generally important affairs or at least for all properly international affairs and problems; a common law of the nations might grow up and international courts to administer it and some kind of system of international police control to maintain and enforce it. In this way, by the general victory of an idea, socialist or other, seeking to organise humanity according to its own model or by any other yet unforeseen way, a sufficient formal unity might come into existence.

The question then arises, how out of this purely formal unity a real psychological unity can be created and whether it can be made a living oneness. For a mere formal, mechanical, administrative, political and economic union does not necessarily create a psychological unity. None of the great empires have yet succeeded in doing that, and even in the Roman where some sense of unity did come into being, it was nothing very close and living; it could not withstand all shocks from within and without, it could not prevent what was much more dangerous, the peril of decay and devitalisation which the diminution of the natural elements of free variation and helpful struggle brought with it. A complete world-union would have indeed this advantage that it would have no need to fear forces from without, for no such forces would any longer exist. But this very absence of outer pressure might well give greater room and power to internal elements of disintegration and still more to the opportunities of decay. It might indeed for a long time foster an internal intellectual and political activity and social progress which would keep it living; but this principle of progress would not be always secure against a natural tendency to exhaustion and stagnation which every diminution of variety and even the very satisfaction of social and economic well-being might well hasten. Disruption of unity would then be necessary to restore humanity to life. Again, while the Roman Empire appealed only to the idea of Roman unity, an artificial and accidental principle, this World-State would appeal to the idea of human unity, a real and vital principle. But if the idea of unity can appeal to the human mind, so too can be idea of separative life, for both address themselves to vital instincts of his nature. What guarantee will there be that the latter will not prevail when man has once tried unity and finds perhaps that its advantages do not satisfy his whole nature? Only the growth of some very powerful psychological factor will make unity necessary to him, whatever other changes and manipulations might be desirable to satisfy his other needs and instincts.

The formal unification of mankind would come in upon us in the shape of a system which would be born, grow, come to its culmination. But every system by the very nature of things tends after its culmination to decay and die. To prevent the organism from decaying and dying there must be such a psychological reality within as will persist a sort of collective national ego which persists through all vital changes. But this ego is not by any means self-existent and immortal; it supports itself on certain things with which it is identified. First, there is the geographical body, the country; secondly, the common interests of all who inhibit the same country, defence, economic well-being and progress, political liberty etc; thirdly, a common name, sentiment culture. But we have to mark that this national ego owes its life to the coalescence of the separative instinct and the instinct of unity; for the nation feels itself one as distinguished from other nations; it owes its vitality to interchange with them and struggle with them in all the activities of its nature. Nor are all these altogether sufficient; there is a deeper factor. There must be a sort of religion of country, a constant even if not always explicit recognition not only of the sacredness of the physical mother, the land, but also, in however obscure a way, of the nation as a collective soul which it is the first duty and need of every man to keep alive, to defend from suppression or mortal attaint or, if suppressed, then to watch, wait and struggle for its release and rehabilitation, if sicklied over with the touch of any fatal spiritual ailment, then to labour always to heal and revivify and save alive.

The World-State will give its inhabitants the great advantages of peace, economic well-being, general security, combination for intellectual, cultural, social activity and progress. None of these are in themselves sufficient to create the thing needed. Peace and security we all desire at present, because we have them not in sufficiency; but we must remember that man has also within him the need of combat, adventure, struggle, almost requires these for his growth and healthy living; that instinct would be largely suppressed by a universal peace and a flat security and it might rise up successfully against suppression. Economic well-being by itself cannot permanently satisfy and the price paid for it might be so heavy as to diminish its appeal and value. The human instinct for liberty, individual and natonal, might well be a constant menace to the World-State, unless it so skilfully arranged its system as to give them sufficient free play. A common intellectual and cultural activity and progress may do much, but need not by themselves be sufficient to bring into being the fully powerful psychological factor that would be required. And the collective ego created would have to rely on the instinct of unity alone, for it would be in conflict with the separative instinct which gives the national ego half its vitality.

It is not impossible that the indispensable inner factor for this outer frame might be increasingly cretead, in its very process of growth, but certain psychological elements would have to be present in great strength. There would be needed, to make the change persist, a religion of humanity or an equivalent sentiment much more powerful, explicit, self-conscious, universal in its appeal than the nationalist's religion of country; the clear recognition by man in all his thought and life of a single soul in humanity of which each man and each people is an incarnation and soul-form; an ascension of man beyond the principle of ego which lives by separativeness,—and yet there must be no destruction of individuality, for without that man would stagnate; a principle and arrangement of the common life which would give free play to the individual variation, interchange in diversity and the need of adventure and conquest by which the soul of man lives and grows great, and sufficient means of expressing all the resultant complex life and growth in a flexible and progressive form of human society.

C. M.K. GANDHI
THE FATHER OF INDIAN NATION

In the modern period M.K. Gandhi is the foremost lover of international peace. Though due to his pre-engagement with the struggle of independence of India he could find little time to visit America or a big part of Europe, but his devotion to the ideal of world peace was immense and intense.

Gandhi was born on 2nd October, 1869 in Porbandar, India. His father Karamchand Gandhi was the Prime Minister of the small state of Porbandar situated in Kathiawar region of India. Though Karamchand Gandhi was the Diwan, he had a fine character and very good conduct. Gandhi has described him objectively as "truthful, brave and generous but shorttempered". Gandhi's mother was Putali Bai. She was extremely religious by temperament. Gandhi inherited excellent qualities of his parents in ample measure.

At nineteen, Gandhi went to England to study law and got his degree of Bar-at-law. In 1891 after getting the degree, he returned to India with an intention of practicing law. In 1893 his law firm sent him to South Africa in connection with a law-suit. There Gandhi got a very degrading and discriminating treatment at the hands of the white government because of his black colour and Indian nationality. In fact such degrading treatment was given to every black person residing in South Africa. But Gandhi was made of different mettle. He decided to fight against this injustice in his own way. He wrote in his autobiography : "The hardship to which I was subjected was only superficial... a symptom of the deep disease of colour prejudice. I should try, if possible, to root out the disease and suffer hardship in the process," And Gandhi did fight against the injustice through a novel technique of non-violence and finally won the battle.

Gandhi was essentially a deeply religious man. But the religion to which he subscribed was not the common man's religion that is "religion not in the sense of subscription to dogmas or conformity to ritual, but religion in the sense of an abiding faith in the absolute values of truth, love and justice and a persistent endeavour to realize them on earth." Gandhi was so intensely religious that he attempted to introduce religion into politics. Historically perhaps Gandhi is the only person who introduced religion into politics so extensively.

Since Gandhi believed in religion having God, it is necessary for us to acquaint ourselves with his concept of God. Gandhi did not believe in any God that divides humanity. According to Gandhi "That Law then which governs all life is God. Law and the Lawgiver are one." To make the point more clear he stated" To me God is Truth and Love; God is ethics and morality; God is fearlessness. God is the source of Light and Life and yet He is above and beyond all these... He transcends speech and reason." But Gandhi went still further when he declared "Truth is God. Man can deny the existence of God; but he cannot deny the existence of Truth."

Gandhi, like a true religious soul, believed that the ultimate ideal of man's life is extinction of ego. So long as one thinks that one is separate from others, one cannot love God. Love implies identification with the Infinite. It implies that the entire creation is one. If one really wants to serve God, one must serve humanity. That is why Gandhi devoted his whole life to the service of mankind, to the service of the lowly and the degraded, to the service of the poor and the havenots.

Because of his religious temperament, Gandhi was of the opinion that no person is entirely bad. Every one is a mixture of good and evill. He is a combination of Dr. Jekyll and Mr. Hyde. But really speaking man being spirit cannot be bad and wicked. That is why Gandhi stated that "there are chords in every human heart. If we only know how to strike the right chord, we bring out the music." Wickedness is therefore not soul-deep. It is a passing phase. Every person can be cured of his wickedness through prayer and wholesome environment. One should not hate the sinner, therefore; one should hate only the sin, and evil that misguides a human soul. That is why Gandhi loved everybody, even his so-called enemy got only his love and not hatred. His political enemies like General Smuts and Jinnah got only sincere affection from Gandhi. The Britishers, against whom Gandhi waged a long battle for liberating India, too got only love and affection of Gandhi.

In order to realize our spiritual self, we need eleven ethical disciplines according to Gandhi. These disciplines are Truth, Non-violence, Brahmacharya (Continence), Tastelessness, Non-stealing, Non-possession, Fearlessness, Removal of untouchability, Bread-labour, Religious tolerance, and Swadeshi. As we have already seen according to Gandhi Truth is God. Non-violence implies complete absence of any illwill or hatred. Gandhi admired simple life. A man of culture is really speaking a man of absolutely simple life. He himself led a very simple life, though power and pelf ran behind him. Gandhi once declared: "I do maintain that asceticism is the greatest of all arts. For what is art but beauty in simplicity, and what is asceticism but the loftiest manifestation of simple beauty in daily life shorn of artificialities and makebelieves. That is why I always say that a true ascetic not only practises art but lives it."

Gandhi had no narrow attitude. Even his concept of Swadeshi did not imply the rejection of others. Swadeshi was defined as "that spirit in us which restricts us to the use and service of our immediate surroundings to the exclusion of the more remote." Human capacity of service is limited. Anybody who pretends to love everybody, must first love the persons residing in his vicinity. An abstract service of abstract humanity has no meaning at all.

Gandhi's view of history too was unique. His interpretation of history can be described as the "non-violent interpretation of history." He declared that history establishes that man has slowly but steadily made progress from that state of cannibalism to a civilized life. One must proceed further to the state of loving every human being if that progress has to be retained.

Gandhi did not accept the materialistic interpretation of history expounded by Marx. Economic factor is no doubt an important factor. But one cannot explain the whole human history on the basis of economic interpretation alone. No permanent good of humanity can be achieved if one believes that violence is the only way to achieve real human progress. Gandhi believed that on the otherhand whatever is achieved through the maximum of violence and bloody conflicts usually and invariably retards real human progress. He wrote: "History teaches one that those who have, no doubt with honest motives, ousted the greedy by using brute force against them, have, in their turn, become a prey to the disease of the conquered."

Gandhi underlined the importance of the individual in bringing about revolution in human mind and human world. He declared "We are the cause and the makers of our surroundings; no body else. To know oneself, to know one's hidden feelings and to correct them is the key to setting right one's surroundings."

To Gandhi state means coersion. Hence he wanted to decentralize the power of the state by making the villages more important. In fact he wrote:

"Self-government means continuous effort to be independent of government control whether it is foreign government or whether it is national." Gandhi did not believe in petty nationalism. He even wished India to die if it became necessary for the svrvival of humanity. He desircd the welfare of all races, all peoples, all religions, all sexes, all colours. He did not like the cult of violence. He was most unhappy at the race of armaments. He very pertinently remarked: "Mankind is at the cross roads. It has to make its choice between the law of the jungle and the law of humanity." In 1939 he urged the democratic powers to accept disarmament voluntarily.

Gandhi wanted that we should make an honest attempt to achieve social progress. For this one must stop running after political power which corrupts human mind. He wrote: "Today politics has become corrupt. Anybody who goes into politics is contaminated. Let us keep out it altogether. Our influence will grow thereby. The greater our inner purity, the greater shall be our hold on the people, without any effort on our part." According to him the methods of social change should be non-cooperation and civil disobedience, and constructive programme. Gandhi himself applied the technique of civil-disobedience and non-cooperation in his struggle against the British Empire and won liberation for India. One must fight through this method against every wrong because thereby no bitterness is produced.

But even more important than civil-disobedience is the constructive programme. Constructive programme has been defined as "construction of Poorna Swaraj or complete Independence by truthful and non-violent means". It included eighteen items viz. Communal Unity, Removal of untouchability, Prohibition, Khadi, other village industries, Village sanitation, New or basic education, Adult education, Women education, Education in health and hygiene, Provincial languages, National language, Economic quality, Kisans, Labour, Adivasis, Lepers and Students. Gandhi made it clear that this is not the final list. One can change it to certain extent, butt he spirit should be kept in mind. In fact Gandhi placed before humanity the ideal of Sarvodaya i.e. the wellbeing of one and all. Our ideal should not be attainment of the greatest good of the greatest number. Our aim should be welfare of all without any exception.

Gandhi advised us to serve human society very sincerely. He said: "I do not want to take power into my hands. By abjuring power and by devoting ourselves to pure and selfless service of the voters, we can guide and influence them. It would give us far more power real power than we shall have by going into the Government."

Gandhi demonstrated through his life how selfless person can achieve much through his sincere efforts even if he is lonely in his pursuit. Our irrational habits find it hard to accept the plea of Gandhi. But we are slowly reaching a stage where there will be no alternative to the Gandhi's way. We shall have to follow him. That will be a glorious day for humanity because then the hour of dawn of human happiness shall come.

Albert Einstein wrote:

"Gandhi is unique in political history. He has invented an entirely new and humane technique for the liberation struggle of an oppressed people and carried it out with the greatest energy and devotion. The moral influence which he has exercised upon thinking people through the civilized world may be far more durable than would appear likely in our present age, with its exaggeration of brute force. For the work of statesmen is permanent only in so far as they arouse and consolidate the moral forces of their peoples through personal example and educating influence.

We are fortunate and should be grateful that fate has bestowed upon us so luminous a contemporary—a beacon to the generations to come." It is not strange that the life of non-violant Gandhi was put to an end by a violent person called Nathuram Godse January 30, 1948 Just as Socrates was unbearable to the ignorant who ruled Greece at that time, Gandhi was unbearable to the violent who rule at present. But Gandhi never said that he was the frail figure that he wore. He was spirit, he was soul. Spirit in immortal. Hence Gandhi too is immortal. In fact New York Times in its issue dated Jan. 31, 1948 stated rightly: "He (Gandhi) has left as his heritage a spiritual force that must in God's good time prevail over arms and armaments and dark doctrines of violence."

WAR OR PEACE ?

It was not without purpose that I reproduced the main parts of Mr. Kirby Page's very able pamphlet on the World War. I hope that the reader followed them with attention the chapters deserved. Mr. Page has proved cnnclusively that both the parties were equally to blame, and that both resorted to barbarous and inhuman practices. We did not need Mr. Page's help to learn that no war of which history has any record took so many lives as this did. Moral loss was greater still. Poisonous forces destructive of the soul (lying and deception) were brought to perfection as much as the forces destructive of the body. The moral results have been as terrible as the physical. It is yet too early to measure the effect on mankind of the collapse of the sexual morality brought about by the War. Vice has usurped the throne of virtue. The brute in man has for the time being gained supremacy.

The after-effects are, perhaps more terrible than the actual and immediate effects. There is no stability about the Government of any single State of Europe. No class is satisfied with its own condition. Each wants to better it at the expanse of the rest. War between the States has now become a war within each State.

India has to make her choice. She may try, if she wishes, the way of war and sink lower than she has. In the Hindu-Muslim quarrel she seems to be taking her first lesson in the art of war. If India can possibly gain her freedom by war, her state will be no better and will be probably much more worse than that of France or England. Past example have become obsolete. Not even Japan's comparative progress can be any guide. For, 'the science' of war has made much greater 'progress' since the Russo-Japanese war. Its result can only be studied in the present condition of Europe. We can safely say that, if India throws off the British yoke by the way of war, she must go through the state Mr. Page has graphically described.

II

But the way of peace is open to her. Her freedom is assured if she has patience. That way will be found to be the shortest even though it may appear to be the longest to our impatient nature. The way of peace insures internal growth and stability. We rejected it because we fancy that it involves submission to the will of the ruler who has imposed himself upon us. But the movement we realize that the imposition is only so called and that, through our unwillingness to suffer loss of life or property, we are party to the imposition, all we need do is to change that negative attitude of passive endorsement. The suffering to be undergone by the change will be nothing compared to the physical suffering and the moral loss we must incur in trying the way of war. And the suffering of war harms both the parties. The sufferings in following the way of peace must benefit both. They will be like the pleasurable travail of a new birth.

Let us not be misled by a hasty generalization of the events of 1920-21. Great as the achievement of that brilliant period was, it was nothing compared to what it might have been, had we been true and had faith. Violence was in the breasts of many of us whilst with our lips we paid homage to non-violence. And though we were thus false to our creed, so far as had accepted it, we blamed it and lost faith instead of blaming and correcting ourselves. Chauri Chaura was a symptom of the disease that was poisoning us. Ours was claimed to be a peaceful, non-violent way. We could not sustain the claim in its fulness. The enemy's taunts we need not mind. They saw violence even where there was not a trace of it. But we could not disregard the judgment of the 'still small voice within'. It knew the violence within.

The way of peace is the way of truth. Truthfulness is even more important than peacefulness. Indeed, lying is the mother of violence. A truthful men cannot long remain violent. He will perceive in the course of his search that he has no need to be violent, and he will further discover that so long as there is the slightest trace of violenee in him, he will fail to find the truth he is searching.

There is no half way between truth and non-violence on the one hand, and untruth and violence on the other. We may never be strong enough to be entirely non-violent in thought, word and deed. But we must keep non-violence as our goal and make steady progress toward it. The attainment of freedom, whether for a man, a nation or the world, must be in exact proportion to the attainment of non-violence by each. Let those, therefore, who believe in non-violence as the only method of achieving real freedom, keep the lamp of non-violence burning bright in the midst of the present impenetrable gloom. The truth of a few will count; the untruth of millions will vanish even like chaff before a whiff of wind.

Young India, 20-5-1926.

'HUMANIZING WAR'

I extract the following interesting paragraphs from an article headed 'War' in the March Number of The Brotherhood :

"Last time the women and children were only starved—it was done by a process cunningly disguised as 'economic pressure'—but next time they are to be gassed to death. Aeroplanes will drop penetrating poisons which will exterminate civil population: Edison says that it should not be difficult to dispose of London's millions in three hours. In every civilized country the chemists are at work searching for some particularly deadly poisons. In England, says Truth, our Government is busy experimenting with improvements in poison gas and killing animals at the rate of two a day in the process. It obtained in one year 689 cats, guinea pigs, goats, mice, monkeys, rabbits and rats, and killed 618 of them with poison gas in search of improvements. "Some idea of the horrors of the next war may be gathered from the fact that the range of guns has been doubled since the Armistice, and that machine guns are now available which fire, 15,00 shots a minute. An automatic cannon will fire one and a quarter pound shells at the rate of 120 a minute, and there is a sixteen-inch gun which hurls a missile weighing more than a ton for a distance of twenty-seven miles. The Chemical Warfare Service in America has discovered a liquid, three drops of which applied to any part of the skin will cause a man's death. One aeroplane, carrying two tons of the liquid, could kill the whole population over miles of territory. General Swinton of the British Army says: 'The great future weapon of war will be deadly germ. We have since the war discovered and developed germs which, dropped down upon cities and armies, will slaughter a nation in a day.

"If anyone is ever in danger of becoming unduly optimistic, let him remember that we spent in 1924 forty millions on education, a hundred and twenty-one millions on armaments, and three hundred and sixteen millions on drink. The business of scientific killing is very expensive, and I am told that nitrogen thrown away in one small and indecisive battle in France would have been enough to save India from a famine. The great world powers are still pouring out incredible amount of their treasure upon armaments, although history so plainly teaches that increasing armaments do nothing but increase the likelihood of wars. Peace-loving America voted eighty-five million dollars for aviation expansion in a few minutes, and no one took the slightest notice of this forward movement in the race for armaments. The irony of the situation is that, while Great Britain is spending nearly twice as much money or armaments to-day as she spent in 1913, the victorious nations have relieved Germany of the burden of such expenditure, so that, in competing with her in industry and commerce, they work under a severe handicap of their own creation."

I add to this the following from The Lancet (June 18,1927):

"Since the arrival of the British troops there have been many cases of influenza and pneumonia, but the question of venereal disease has been the most clamant one, and in spite of every possible precaution the number of those affected has steadily increased... A number of prostitutes from North and South have flocked to Shanghai, most of them being Chinese (6 per cent), Russian (30 per cent), and Japanese (5 per cent). The majority of the brothels are in the French Concession and in Chinese districts bordering on municipal roads. The high venereal rate has given the Command much concern, and no stone is left unturned in the effort to lower it."

And yet there are intelligent men who talk, and gullible men who subscribe to the talk, of the 'humanizing influence' of war.

Young India, 11-8-1927.

THE DOOM OF PFACE

(Gandhiji's message cabled to the Editor of the Cosmopolitan New York, at the commencement of the Italian invasion.)

Not to believe in the possibility of permanent peace is to

disbelieve in godliness of human nature. Methods hitherto adopted have failed because rock-bottom sincerity on the part of those who have striven has been lacking. Not that they have realized this lack. Peace is unattainable by part performance of conditions, even as chemical combination is impossible without complete fulfilment of conditions of attainment thereof. If recognized leaders of mankind who have control over engines of destruction were wholly to renounce their use with full knowledge of implications, permanent peace can be obtained. This is clearly impossible without the great powers of the earth renouncing their imperialistic designs. This again seem impossible without these great nations ceasing to believe in soul-destroying competition and to desire to multiply wants and therefore increase their material possessions. It is my conviction that the root of the evil is want of a living faith in a living God. It is a first-class human tragedy that peoples of the earth who claim to believe in the message of Jesus whom they describe as the Prince of Peace show little of that belief in actual practice. It is painful to see sincere Christian divines limiting the scope of Jesus's message to select individuals. I have been taught from my childhood, and I have tested the truth by experience, that primary virtues of mankind are possible of cultivation by the meanest of the human species. It is this undoubted universal possibility that distinguishes the human from the rest of God's creation. If even one great nation were unconditionally to perform the supreme act of renunciation, many of us would see in our lifetime visible peace established on earth.

Harijan, 16-5-1936

GOD OF LOVE, NOT WAR

The Statesman of Delhi has devoted four articles to an unmeasured condemnation of the no-war movement led by Canon Sheppard and other earnest Christians in England. The paper has dragged into its support the authority of the Bhagavadgita in these words:

> "Indeed the true but difficult teaching of Christianity seems to be that society must fight its enemies but love them. Such, too,—will Mr. Gandhi please note—is the clear teaching

of the Bhagavadgita, where Krishna tells Arjuna that victory also goes to him who fights with complete fearlessness and is utterly devoid of hatred. Indeed, on the highest plane the argument between conscientious objector and the knightly warrior is for ever settled in the second book of that great classic. We have little space to quote, and the whole poem deserves to be read not once but many times."

The writer of the articles perhaps does not know that the terrorist has also used in his defence the very verses quoted by him. But the fact is that a dispassionate reading of the Bhagavadgita has revealed to me a meaning wholly contrary to the one given to it by the Statesman writer. He has forgotten that Arjuna was no conscientious objector in the sense the Western wa-resisters are. Arjuna believed in war. He had fought the Kaurava hosts many times before. But he was unnerved when the two armies were drawn up in battle array and when he suddenly realized that he had to fight his nearest kinsmen and revered teachers. It was not love of man or the hatred of war that had actuated the questioner. Krishna could give no other answer than he did. The immortal author of the Mahabharata, of which the Gita is one—no doubt the brighest—of the many gems contained in that literary mine, has shown to the world the futility of war by giving the victors an empty glory, leaving but seven victors alive out of the millions said to have been engaged in the fight in which unnamable atrocities were used on either side. But the Mahabharata has a better message even than the demonstration of war as a delusion and folly. It is the spiritual history of man considered as an immortal being and has used with a magifying lens a historical episode considered in his times of moment for the tiny world round him, but in terms of present-day values of no significance. In those days the globe had not shrunk to a pinhead, as it has today, on which the slightest movement on one spot affects the whole. The Mahabharata depicts for all time the eternal struggle that goes on daily between the forces of good and evil in the human breast and in which though good is ever victorious evil does put up a brave show and baffles even the keenest conscience. It shows also the only way to right action.

But whatever the true message of the Bhagavadgita may be, what matters to the leaders of the peace movement is not what the Gita says, but what the Bible, which is their spiritual dictionary, says, and then too not what meaning the Church authorities give to it, but, what meaning a prayerful reading of it yields to the reader. What matters most of all is objector's knowledge of the law of love or ahimsa, inadequately rendered in English as non-violence. The articles of the Statesman are perhaps a fair challange to the objectors. I am sorry I do not know enough of the movement to give a definite opinion. My opinion need have no weight whatsoever with the objectors. But it has, inasmuch as I know intimately some of them who even correspond with me. And now they have gone a step further in that they have adopted almost as their text-book. Mr. Richard Gregg's book called The Power of Nonviolence which is claimed by its author to be a Western interpretation of what non-violence as I interpret it, stands for. It may not, therefore, be presumptuous on my part, if I set down without argument the implications and conditions of the success of non-violence. Here they are:

(1) Non-violence is the law of the human race and is infinitely greater than and superior to brute force.

(2) In the last resort it does not avail to those who do not possess a living faith in the God of Love.

(3) Non-violence affords the fullest protection to one's self-respect and sense of honour, but not always to possession of land or movable property, though its habitual practice does prove a better bulwark than the possession of armed men to defend them. Non-violence, in the very nature of things, is of no assistance in the defence of ill-gotten gains and immoral acts.

(4) Individuals or nation who would practise non-violence must be prepared to sacrifice (nations to the last man) their all except honour. It is, therefore, inconsistent with the possession of other people's countries, i.e., modern imperialism, which is frankly based on force for its defence.

(5) Non-violence is a power which can be wielded equally by all-children, young men and women or grown-up people, provided they have a living faith in the God of Love and therefore equal love for all mankind. When non-violence is accepted as the law of life it must prevade the whole being and not be applied to isolated acts.

(6) It is a profound error to suppose that whilist the law is good enough for individuals it is not for masses of mankind.

Harijan, 5-9-1936

WHY NOT GREAT POWERS ?

In the criticism of my recent writings on the plight of Czechoslovakia, I have observed one thing which demands an answer.

Some critics argue that, if the non-violent remedy I have suggested for the Czechs is only for comparatively weak because small nations like them and not for the great powers like England or Fance or Amrrica, it cannot be of much value, if any.

Now if the critics will re-read my article, they will see that I have refrained from suggesting it to these big powers because of their bigness, in other words, because of my timidity. But there was a more potent reason for my not addressing them. They were not in distress and therefore in no need of any remedy. To use a medical expression, they were not ailing as Czechoslovakia was. Their existence was not threatened, as Czechoslovakia's was. Any appeal from me, therefore, to the great powers would have amounted to an empty and unwanted sermon. By experience I have also found that people rarely become virtuous for virtue's sake. They become virtuous from necessity. Nor is there anything wrong in a man becoming good under pressure of circumstances. It would be no doubt better, if he becomes good for its own sake. The Czechs were given a choice either to surrender peacefully to Germany's might or to fight single-handed and risk almost certain destruction. It was at this moment that it became necessary for one like me to present an alternative which had proved its effectiveness under somewhat similar circumstances. My appeal to the Czechs was, in my opinion, as appropriate as it would have been appropriate in the case of the great powers.

My critics might have, however, well asked why I had gone out of my self-prescribed orbit to speak to a Western nation when I could not show cent percent success of non-violence on the Indian soil-more especially now, when I had begun to entertain serious doubts as to whether Congressmen were really living up to their creed or policy of non-violence. Indeed I had in mind the limitation and the present state of uncertainty about the Congress position. But my own faith in the non-violent remedy was as bright as ever when I wrote that article. And I felt that in the supreme hour of its trial it would be cowardly on my part not to suggest to the Czechs the non-violent remedy for acceptance. What may ultimately prove impossible of acceptance by crores of people, undisciplined, and unused till but recently to corporate suffering, might be possible for a small, compact, disciplined nation inured to corporate suffering. I had no right to arrogate to myself any belief that India alone and no other nation was fit for non-violent action. I must confess that I have believed and still believe that India was the fittest nation to enforce non-violent action for regaining her freedom. In spite of signs to the contrary, I have the hope that the whole mass of people, who are more than the Congress, will respond only to non-violent action. They are the readiest of all the nations of the earth for such action. But when a case for immediate application of the remedy presented itself before me, I could not restrain myself from suggesting it to the Czechs for their acceptance.

It is, however, open to the great powers to take it up any day and cover themselves with glory and earn eternal gratitude of posterity. If they or any of them can shed the fear of destruction, if they disarm themselves, they will automatically help the rest to regain their sanity. But then these great powers have to give up imperialistic ambitions and exploitation of the so-called uncivilized or semi-civilized nations of the earth and revise their mode of life. It means a complete revolution. Great nations can hardly be expected in the ordinary course to move spontaneously in a direction the reverse of the one they have followed and, according to their notion of value, from victory to victory. But miracles have happened before and may happen even in this very prosaic age. Who can dare limit God's power of undoing wrong? One thing is certain. If the mad race for armaments continues, it is bound to result in a slaughter such as has never occurred in his. If there is a victor left, the very victory will be a living death for the nation that emerges victorious. There is no escape from the impending doom save through a bold and unconditional acceptance of the non-violent method with all its glorious implications. Democracy and violence can ill go together. The States that ars today nominally democratic have either to become frankly totalitarian or, if they are to become truly democratic, they must become courageously non-violent. It is a blasphemy to say that non-violence can only be practised by individuals and never by nations which are composed by individuals.

Peshawar 5-11-38
Harijan, 12-11-1938

ON ITS TRIAL

"I am a pacifist still in one sense; that is to say, I realize that Christians should be able to meet material force with spiritual power. It is horrifying to reflect that after nineteen hundred years, we are still unable to do it except in individual cases and on a small scale. But to me it seems merely 'wishful thinking' to act as though we had a power which in fact we have not and for which we have neither trained nor disciplined ourselves in the past. Such power does not come to those who have not disciplined themselves, at the last moment, in the hour of need. It has not come to us. I would rather, therefore, do what I can in defence of principles which I believe to be both right in themselves and of enormous importance to the future of the human race, than stand aside and do nothing. It is doing nothing that is the worst expedient of all.

When, therefore, my pacifist friends ask me whether I can imagine Jusus Christ droping a bomb or firing a gun I am entitled to reply: 'No, I cannot; but neither can I imagine him standing aside and doing nothing at all'.

I am compelled to echo the words of a very dear relative of mine who, loathing was as much as any pacifist that ever breathed, said to me at the beginning of the last war (in which he lost his life): 'If you can stop war with spiritual power, do it. If you can't, let me do what I can; and if you are right in thinking that war is so damnable that anyone who takes part in it is damned, then I would rather be damned than let these things go on without doing all I can to stop them, even at the cost of my life'.

Is this not very close to the meaning of our Lord when he said: 'He that loseth his life shall save it?'

The foregoing is the concluding portion of a touchingly sorrowful article contributed to The Survey Graphic of December 1941 by the celebrated Dr. Maude Royden of the Guildhouse London. She is one of the foremost pacifists of the West. Like many she felt compelled to revise her position and is now most reluctantly but fully ranged on the side of the defenders of the British Isles.

The article demands a considered reply, I have been in constant touch with the Western pacifists. In my opinion Dr. Royden has surrendered her position in the portion I have quoted. If the individuals have lived up to the Christian teaching (i.e. on non-violence) and that on a small scale, one would think practice should make such a life possible for many people and on a large scale. It is undoubtedly wrong and foolish "to act as though one had the power which in fact one has not". "But", says the worthy writer, "such power does not come to those who have not disciplined themselves, at the last moment, in the hour of need".

I suggest that with the knowledge of the defect no time should be lost in seeking to remove it. That by itself is doing not only something but the right thing. To deny one's faith by contrary practice is surely the worst thing one can do.

And I am not sure that "doing nothing is the worst expedient of all". In septic treatment, for instance, doing nothing is not only expedient, it is obligatory.

There is no cause whatsoever for despondency, much less for denial of one's faith at the crucial moment. Why should not British pacifist stand aside and remodel their life in its entirety? They might be unable to bring about peace outright, but they would lay a solid foundation for it and give the surest test of their faith. When, in the face of an upheaval such as we are witnessing, there are only a few individuals of immovable faith, they have to live up to their faith even though they may produce no visible effect on the course of events. They should believe that their aation will produce tangible results in due course. Their staunchness is bound to attract sceptics. I would also suggest that individuals like Dr. Maude Royden are not mere camp followers. They are leaders. Therefore, they have to live their lives in strict accord with the Sermon on the Mount, and they will find immediately that there is much to give up and much to remodcl. The greatest thing that they have to deny themselves is the fruit of imperialism. The present complicated life of tbe Londoner and his high living is possible only because of the hoards brought from Asia, Africa and other parts of the world. In spite of the fierce criticism which has been levelled against my letter 'To Every Briton', I adhere to every word of it, and I am convinced that posterity will adopt the remedy suggested therein against violence, however, organized and fierce. And now that the enemy is at the gates of India I am advising the countrymen the same course of action I advised the British people. My advice may or may not be accepted by my countrymen. I would remain unmoved. Their non-acceptance will be no test of failure of non-violence. I would subscribe to the charge of my imperfection. But a satyagrahi does not wait for perfection before he invites other to experiment with him, provided always that his faith is immovable like a mountain. The adivce that Dr. Royden's relative gave her and which she quotes approvingly is altogether wrong. If the war is damnable, how can he stop the things that go on by taking part in it, even though it may be on the defensive side and at the cost of his own life? For the defence has to resort to all the damnable things that the enemy does, and that with greater vigour if it has to succeed. Such a giving of life is not saving it but a mere waste.

I have attended the Doctor's services in her Church where a living belief in the efficiency of prayer is much in vogue. When the impenetrable gloom surrounded her, why did she not find strength and consolation and real action in heart-prayer? It is never too late to mend. She and her fellow-pacifists, many of whom I have the privilege of knowing, should take heart and, like Peter, repent of the momentary loss of faith and return to the old faith in non-violence with renewed vigour. Their return will mean no material loss to the war effort but will mean a great deal to the anti-war effort, which is bound to succeed sooner rather later, if man is to live as man and not become a two-footed brute.

Sevagram, 8-3-42
Harijan, 15-3-1942

WORKING OF NON-VIOLENCE

What is happening today is disregard of the law of non-violence and enthronement of violence as if were an eternal law. The democracies, therefore, that we see at work in England, America and France are only so-called, because they are no less based on violence than Nazi Germany, Fascist Italy or even soviet Russia. The only difference is that the violence of the last three is much better organized than that of the three democratic powers. Nevertheless we see today a mad race for outdoing one another in the matter of armaments. And if, when the clash comes, as it is bound to come one day, the democracies win, they will do so only because they will have the backing of their peoples who imagine that they have a voice in their own government, whereas in the other three cases the peoples might rebel against their own dictatorships.

Holding the view that without the recognition of non-violence on a national scale there is no such thing as a constitutional or democratic government, I devote my energy to the propagation of non-violence as the law of our life-individual, social, political, national and international. I fancy that I have seen the light, though dimly. I write cuatiously, for I do not profess to know the whole of the law. If I know the successes of my experiments, I know also my failures. But the successes are enough to fill me with undying hope.

I have often said that, if one takes care of the means, the end will take care of itself. Non-violence is the means; the end for every nation is complete independence. There will be an international league only when all the nations, big or small, composing it are fully independent. The nature of that independence will correspond to the extent of non-violence assimilated by the nations concerned. One thing is certain. In a society based on non-violence, the smallest nation will feel as tall as the tallest. The idea of superiority and inferiority will be wholly obliterated. ....

Sevagram, 6-2-1939
Harijan, 11-2-1939

....

A Friendly Overture

TO END WAR

The conversation then turned on the question of war.

"How to you think the succession of wars such as we have witnessed of late can be stopped?" he (a Director of an influential British daily paper) asked.

"I have no doubt," replied Gandhiji, "that unless big nations shed their desire of exploitation and the spirit of violence of which war is the natural expression and atom bomb the inevitable consequence, there is no hope for peace in the world. I tried so speak out during the war and wrote open letters to the British people, to Hitler and to the Japanese and was dubbed a fifth columnist for my pains."

Sodepur, 30-10-1946
Harijan, 10-11-1946

STRIVE FOR ONE WORLD

"I will not like to live in this world if it is not to be one. Certainly I should like to see this dream realized in my lifetime," declared Gandhlji in answer to a question whether he believed in the theory of one world and whether it would succeed under the present conditions.

He added: "I hope that all the representatives who have come here from the different Asian countries will strive their level best to have only one world. They will have to think out ways and means for achieving this goal.

"If you work with fixed determination, there is no doubt that in our own generation we will certainly realize this dream."

Harijan, 20-4-1947

TO EVERY BRITON

"...Your statesmen have deelared that this is a war on behalf of democracy. There are many reasons given in justification. You know them all by heart. I suggest that at the end of the war, whichever way it ends, there will be no democracy left to represent democracy. This war has descended upon mankind as a curse and a warning. It is a curse inasmuch as it is brutalizing man on a scale hitherto unknown. All distinctions between comtantants and non-combatanta have been abolished. No one and nothing is to be spared. Lying has been reduced to an art...... It is a warning that, if nobody reads the writing on the wall. Man will be reduced to the state of the beast, whom he is shaming by his manners......

I appeal for cessation hostilities, not because you are too exhausted to fight, but because war is bad in essence. You want to kill Nazism. You will never kill it by its indifferent adoption. Your soldiers are doing the same work of destruction as the Germans. The only difference is that perhaps your are not as thorough as the Germans. If that be so, yours will soon acquire the same thoroughness as theirs, if not much greater. On no other condition can you win the war. In other words, you will have to be more ruthless than the Nazis. No cause, however, just, can warrant the indiscriminate slaughter that is going minute by minute. I suggest that a cause that demands the inhumanities that are being perpetrated to-day cannot be called just.........

I venture to present you with a nobler and braver way, worthy of the bravest soldier. I want you to fight Nazism without arms, or if I am to retain the military terminology, with non-violent arms......"

New Delhi, 2-7-1940
Harijan, 6-7-1940

ON PATRIOTISM

"...Just as the cult of patriotism teaches us today that the individual has to die for the family, the family has to die for the village, the village for the district, the district for the province, the province for the country, even so, a country has to be free in order that it may die, if necessary, for the benefit of the world. My love therefore of nationalism, or my idea of nationalism, is that my country may become free, that if need be, the whole country may die, so that the human race may live..."

—*Gandhiji in Indian Villages*, by Mahadev Desai, Madras, 1927, p. 170

"Isolated independence is not the goal of the world states. It is voluntary interdependence."

—*Young India*, 17-7-1924

"There is no limit to extending our services to our neighbours across State-made frontiers. God never made those frontiers."

—*Young India*, 31-12-31

D. JAWAHARLAL NEHRU
LATE-PRIME MINISTER OF INDIA

Pandit Jawaharlal Nehru was not only the political heir of Mahatma Gandhi, the Father of Indian Nation, he was a thinker and democrat of the first order. He was a great humanist and said "The moment we forget the human approach, somehow the foundation of our thinking is removed."

On another occasion he spoke about the fact that "national isolation is neither a desirable nor a possible ideal in a world which is daily becoming more of a unit."

He was a great advocate of world peace and declared "Peace and freedom have become indivisible and the world cannot continue for long partly free and partly subject."

It is worthwhile to recall that according to Nehru, "The question of peace becomes of paramount importance of this world of ours is to make progress or indeed even survive."

PROBLEMS OF PEACE

I have listened attentively and with respect to many of the speeches made here, and sometimes I have felt as if I was being buffeted by the icy winds of the cold war. Coming from a warm country, I have shivered occasionally at these cold blasts.

Speaking here in this assembly chamber, an old memory comes back to me. In the fateful summer of 1938, I was a visitor at a meeting of the League of Nations in Geneva. Hitler was advancing then and holding out threats of war. There was mobilization in many parts of Europe, and the tramp of armed men was being heard. Even so, the League of Nations appeared to be unconcerned and discussed all manner of subjects, except the most vital subject of the day. The war had not started then. A year later it descended upon the world with all its thunder and destructive fury. After many years of carnage, the war ended and a new age—the atomic age—was ushered in by the terrible experience of Hiroshima and Nagasaki.

Fresh from these horrors, the minds of men turned to thoughts of peace, and there was a passionate desire to put an end to war itself. The United Nations took birth on a note of high idealism embodied in the noble wording of the Charter. But there was also a realization of the state of the postwar world as it was. Therefore, provision was made in the structure of the organization to balance certain conflicting urges. There were permanent members of the Security Council and there was provision for unanimity amongst the great powers. All this was not very logical. But it represented certain realities of the world as it was, and because of this, we accepted them.

At that time, large areas in Asia and even more so in Africa were not represented in the United Nations and they were under colonial domination. Since then the colonial part of the world has shrunk greatly, and we now welcome here many countries from Africa in their new freedom. The United Nations has become progressively more representative. But we must remember that, even now, it is not fully so. Colonialism still has its strong footholds in some parts of the world, and racialism and racial domination are still prevalent, more especially in Africa.

During these past fifteen years, the United Nations has often been criticized for its structure and for some of its activities. These criticisms have had some justification behind them. But, looking at the broad picture, I think we can definitely say that the United Nations has amply justified its existence and repeatedly prevented the recurrent crises from developing into war. It has played a great role, and it is a little difficult now to think of this troubled world without the U.N.O. If it had defects, they lay in the world situation itself which inevitably mirrored. If there had been no United Nations today, our first task would be to create something of that kind. I should like, therefore, to pay my tribute to the work of the United Nations as a whole, even though I might criticize some aspect of it from time to time.

The structure of the United Nations, when it started, was weighted in favour of Europe and the Americas. It did not seem to us to be fair to the countries of Asia and Africa. But we appreciated the difficulties of the situation and did not press for any changes. With the growth of the United Nations and more countries coming in, its structure today has become still more unbalanced. Even so, we wish to proceed slowly and with agreement with not to press for any change which would involve an immediate amendment of the Charter and the raising of heated controversies.

Unfortunately, we live in a split world which is constantly coming up against the basic assumptions of the United Nations. We have to bear with this and try to move even more forward to the conception of full co operation between nations. That co operation does not and must not mean any domination of one country by another, any coercion or compulsion forcing a country to line with another country. Each country has something to give and something to take from others. The moment coercion is exerted on a country, not only is its freedom impaired, but its growth suffers.

We have to acknowledge that there is great diversity in the world and that this variety is good and is to be encouraged, so that each country may grow and its creative impulse might have full play in accordance with its own genius. Hundreds and thousands of years of history have conditioned us in our respective countries, and our roots go deep down into the soil. If these roots are pulled out, we wither. If these roots remain strong and we allow the winds from four quarters to blow in upon us, they will yield branch and flower and fruit.

Many of the speakers from this forum have surveyed the world scene and spoken on a variety of problems. I would like to concentrate on what I consider the basic problem of all. My mind is naturally filled with problems of my own country and our passionate desire to develop and to put an end to the poverty and low standards of living which have been a curse to hundreds of millions of our people. To that end we are labouring, as indeed other underdeveloped countries are doing. Even so, there is something else which we consider is of greater importance. That is peace. Without peace all our dreams vanish and are reduced to ashes. The Charter of the United Nations declares our determination to save succeeding generations from the scourge of war to reaffirm faith in fundamental human rights, and for these ends to practise tolerance and live together in peace with one another as good neighbours.

The main purpose of the United Nations is to build up a world without war, a world based on the co-operation of nations and peoples. It is not merely a world where war is kept in check by a balancing of armed forces. It is much deeper than that. It is world from which the major causes of war have been removed with social structures built up which further peaceful co-operation within a nation as well as between nations.

In the preamble of the constitution of UNESCO it is stated that 'war begins in the minds of men'. That is essentially true; and ultimately it is necessary to bring about the change in our minds and to remove fears and apprehensions, hatreds and suspicions. Disarmament is a part of this process, for it will create an atmosphere of cooperation. But it is only a step towards our objective, a part of the larger efforts to rid the world of war and the causes of war.

In the present context, however, disarmament assumes a very special importance for us, overriding all other issues. For many years past, there have been talks on disarmament and some progress has undoubtedly been made in so far as the plans and proposals are concerned. Still we find that the race of armaments continues, as also the efforts to invent ever more powerful engines of destruction. If even a small part of these efforts was directed to the search for peace, probably the problem of disarmament would have been solved by this time.

Apart from the moral imperative of peace, every practical consideration leads us to that conclusion. For, as everyone knows, the choice today in this nuclear age is one of utter annihilation and destruction of civilization or of some way to have peaceful co-existence between nations. There is no middle way. If war is an abomination and an ultimate crime which has to be avoided, we must fashion our minds and policies accordingly. There may be risks, but the greatest risk is to allow the present dangerous drift to continue. In order to achieve peace we have to develop a climate of peace and tolerance and to avoid speech and action which tend to increase fear and hatred.

It may not be possible to reach full disarmament in one step, though every step should be conditioned to that end. Much ground has already been covered in the discussions on disarmament But the sands of time run out, and we dare not play about with this issue or delay its consideration. This, indeed, is the main duty of the United Nations today and if it fails in this, the United Nations fails in its main purpose.

We live in an age of great revolutionary changes brought about by the advance of science and technology. Therein lies the hope for the world and also the danger of sudden death. Because of these advances, the time we have for controlling the forces of destruction is strictly limited.

In the context of things as they are today, the great nations, the United States of America and the Soviet Union, hold the key to war and peace. Theirs is a great responsibility. But every country, big or small, is concerned in this matter of peace and war and, therefore, every country must shoulder its responsibility and work to this end. In order to deal with these issues effectively, we have to take earnest and impersonal views. It is only the United Nations as a whole that can ultimately solve these problems. Therefore, while all efforts towards disarmament must be welcomed, the United Nations should be closely associated with such efforts.

The question of disarmament has been considered at various levels. There is the question of general disarmament, and of the ending of test explosions of nuclear and thermonuclear weapons. So far as test explosins are concerned, considerable progress has been made in the discussions of the committee which has been meeting in Geneva. Indeed, it would appear that an agreement has been reached on many basic issues and only a little more effort is needed to complete this agreement. I suggest that a final agreement on this subject should be reached as early as possible. This is not, strictly speaking, disarmament, but undoubtedly any such agreement will bring a large measure of relief to the world. Disarmament must include the prohibition of the manufacture, storage and use of weapons of mass destruction, as well as the progressive limitation of conventional weapons.

It is admitted that disarmament should take place in such stages as to maintain broadly the balance of armed power. It is only on this basis that success can be achieved and this pervading sense of fear countered. It must also be clearly understood that disarmament and a machinery for control must go together, and neither of these can be taken up singly.

A proposal has been made that the question of disarmament should be referred to a committee of experts. In fact, experts have been considering this matter during the past years, and we have had the advantage of their views. A reference to a committee of experts should not lead to a postponement of the major issue. Any such delay may well be disastrous. Possibly, while the major issues are being considered by the United Nations Commission or other committees, a reference of any special aspect might be made to the experts. What is important is that the United Nations, at the present juncture, should ensure that there is adequate machinery for promoting disarmament and that this machinery should function continuously.

The fear of surprise attacks or accidental happenings leading to dangerous developments is undoubtedly present in the existing situation. The best way to deal with this fear is to reduce international tension and create an atmosphere which will make it very difficult for any surprise attack to take place. In addition, such other steps as may be considered necessary for prevention of surprise attacks should be taken. If there is an agreement on the stoppage of nuclear tests and use of carriers, immediately danger from surprise attacks will be greatly lessened.

While disarmament is by far the most urgent problem and brooks no delay, we have to face today a situation in Africa, in the Congo, which has led the United Nations to assume heavy and novel responsibilities. Everyone present here, I am sure, warmly welcomes the coming of independence to many parts of Africa, to many peoples there who have suffered untold agony for ages past. We wish them well, and the United Nations has shown its readiness to help them in various ways.

There are three aspects of this African problem: firstly, full implementation of the independence and freedom that have been achieved; secondly, liberation of those countries in Africa which are still under colonial domination. This has become an urgent task. Today some of these countries are almost cut off from the outside world, and even news is not allowed to reach us. From such accounts as we have, the fate of the people in these countries is even worse than that in the other countries of Africa. Thridly, there is the question of some countries in Africa which are independent but where that freedom is confined to a minority, and where the great majority have no share in it and, indeed, are suppressed politically, socially and racially in defiance of everything that the United Nations and the world community stand for. Racialism and the doctrine of a master race dominating over others can be tolerated no longer and can only lead to vast racial conflicts.

The recent developments in Africa have indicated the great danger of delay in dealing with these problems. It is not possible any longer to maintain colonial domination in any of the countries, and I think it is the duty and basic responsibility of the United Nations to expedite their freedom. There is a tremendous ferment all over the continent of Africa. This has to be recognized and appreciated and met with foresight and wisdom.

The question of the Republic of the Congo has especially

come before us. The first thing that strikes one is the utter failure of a colonial system which left the Congo in its present state. Long years of colonial rule resulted in extracting vast wealth from that country for the enrichment of the colonial power, while the people of the country remained utterly poor and backward. The situation there is a complicated and frequently changing one, and it is not always easy to know what is happening. Disruptive forces have been let loose and have been encouraged by people who do not wish this newly independent Congo well. Some footholds of the old colonialism are still engaged in working to this end. It is an encouragement to the disruption of the State. We must realize that it is essential to maintain the integrity of the Congo, for if there is disintegration of the State, that is bound to lead to internal civil wars on a large scale. There will be no peace in the Congo except on the basis of the integrity of the State. Foreign countries must particularly avoid any interference in its internal affairs or encouragement of one faction against another.

The role of the United Nations is a mediatory one, to reconcile and help in the proper functioning of the Central Government. Help in the development of the Congo is again a tremendous and long-term problem. Ultimately, it is the people of the Congo who will have to produce their own leadership, whether it is good or bad. Leadership cannot be imposed, and any attempt to do so will lead to conflict. The United Nations obviously cannot act all the time as policemen, nor should any outside power intervene.

There is an elected parliament in the Congo, though it does not appear to be functioning. It should be the function of the United Nations to help the country's parliament to meet and function so that out of its deliberations the problem of the Congo may be dealt with by the people themselves. The decisions must be those of parliament as representing the people of the Congo, and not of others. The functioning of parliament may itself lead to the ironing out of internal differences.

I hope that it will be possible soon for the Congo to take its place in this Assembly. The Security Council has repeatedly laid stress on Belgiam military personnel leaving the Congo. These decisions have apparently not been given full effect to.

This is highly undersirable. It seems to me of great importance, both in view of past history and present conditions, that every type of military or semi-military personnel of Belgium should leave the Congo. The General Assembly might well consider sending a delegation to the Congo to find out what foreign troops or other personnel, apart from those sent on behalf of the United Nations, are still there, and how far they are interfering in local affairs.

Recently an emergency session of the General Assembly considered the situation in the Congo and made certain suggestions. The resolution of the emergency session has rightly indicated the broad lines of approach and the basic principles laid down in it should be implemented. The problem of the development of a huge country has also become partly the responsibility of the United Nations. These responsibilities cannot be shirked, and it may have to be considered how best to shoulder these responsibilities.

Two aspects have to be borne in mind. Broad policies in these grave matters must be laid down by the General Assembly or by the Security Council. In so far as executive action is concerned, it would not be desirable for the executive to be weakend when frequent and rapid decision have to be made. That would mean an abdication of the responsibilities undertaken by the United Nations. If the executive itself is split and pulls in different directions, it will not be able to function adequately or with speed. For that reason, the executive should be given authority to act within the terms of directions issued. At the same time, the executive has to keep in view all the time the impact of various forces in the world. The Secretary-General might well consider what organizational steps should be taken to deal adequately with this novel situation.

It has been suggested that some structural changes should take place in the United Nations. Probably some changes would be desriable because of the emergence of many independent countries in Asia and Africa. But my attempt at bringing about these changes by an amendment of the Charter at the present juncture is likely to raise many controversial questions and thus add greatly to the difficulties we face. It should be possible for us even within the terms of the Charter to adapt the

United Nations machinery to meet situations as they arise, more especially in view of the increasing responsibilities of the United Nations.

If, as I earnestly hope, disarmament makes progress, the United Nations will come into another domain of vast responsibility which will have to be discharged. Possibly, special commissions working under the umbrellas of the United Nations might be charged with this task.

I do not propose to deal with many other matters here. But, in view of a controversy that is at present going on in the General Assembly, I should like to refer briefly to the question of proper representation of China in the United Nations. For a number of years India has brought this issue before the United Nations because we have felt not only that it is improper for that great and powerful country to remain unrepresented, but that this has an urgent bearing on all world problems and especially those of disarmament. We hold that all countries must be represented in the U.N. We have welcomed during this session many new countries. It appears most extraordinary that any argument should be advanced to keep out China and to give the seat meant for China to those who certainly do not and cannot represent China. It is well known that we Indians have had, and are having, a controversy with the People's Government of China over our northern frontier. In spite of that controversy we continue to feel that proper representation of the People's Republic in the U.N. is essential; the longer we delay it, the more harm we cause to the U.N. and to the consideration of the major problems we have before us.

In this connection, I should like to mention another country—Mongolia. When we are rightly admitting so many countries to the U.N., why should Mongolia be left out? What wrong has it done, what violation of the Charter? Here are a quiet and peaceful people working hard for their progress, and it seems to me utterly wrong from any point of principle to exclude them from this great organization. India has a special sentiment in regard to Mongolia, because our relations with that country go back into the distant past of more than fifteen hundred years. Even now there are many evidences of those old contacts and friendly relations between the two countries. I would earnestly recommend that Mongolia should be accepted in this World Assembly of Nations.

There is one other matter to which I should like to refer. That is Algeria. It has been a pain and a torment to many of us in Asia, in Africa and possibly elsewhere, to witness this continuing tragedy of a brave people fighting for their freedom. Many arguments have been advanced and many difficulties pointed out. But the basic fact is that people have struggled continuously for years at tremendous sacrifice and against heavy odds to attain independence. Once or twice it appeared that the struggle might end satisfactorily in freedom by exercise of the principle of self-determination. But the moments slipped by, and the tragedy continued, I am convinced that every country in Asia and Africa and, I believe, many countries in other continents also are deeply concerned over this matter and hope earnestly that this terrible war will end soon bringing freedom to the Algerian people. This is an urgent problem to which the United Nations must address itself in order to bring about an early solution.

I do believe that the vast majority of the people in every country want us to labour for peace and to succeed. Whether we are big or small, we have to face big issues vital to the future of humanity. Everything else is of lesser importance than this major question. I am absolutely convinced that we shall never settle this question by war or by a mental approach which envisages war and prepares for it.

I am equally convinced that if we aim at right ends, right means must be employed. Good will not emerge out of evil methods. That was the lesson which our great leader Gandhi taught us, and though we in India have failed in many ways in following his advice, something of his message still clings to our minds and hearts. In ages long past a great son of India, the Buddha, said that the only real victory was one in which all were equally victorious and there was defeat for no one. In the world today that is the only practical victory. Any other way will lead to disaster.

It is therefore, this real victory of peace in which all are winners that I would like this great Assembly to keep before its mind and to endeavour to achieve.

E. DR. S. RADHAKRISHNAN

Dr. Radhakrishnan was a very impressive exponent of Indian philosophy. He was a very brilliant thinker. He was a democrat with a difference because according to him "Essentially, a domocrat is one who has that trait of humanity, the power to put himself in the second place, to believe that he may possibly be mistaken and his opponent probably right."

He refuses to accept nationalism as a natural instinct. He calls it 'an acquired artificial emotion' and adds that "man as he is, need not be regarded as the crowning glory of evolution". He is of the opinion that "the next stage of evolution is not in man's physique but in his psyche, in his mind and spirit, in the emergence of a larger understanding and awareness, in the development of a new integration of character adequate to the new age."

He is of the opinion that for a true and peaceful world-order people must attain true understanding and realize that "the differences need not be fused, but they need not conflict". He thinks that peace can be attained only if spiritual progress is realised.

PARLIAMENTARY DEMOCRACY

I find myself in the Chair today owning to the regrettable absence of Shri G. V. Malvalankar on account of serious illness. He has had long and large experience of parliamentary procedures and would have given you effective guidance.

It is wise for us sometimes to detach ourselves from the rough and tumble of active politics and consider the foundations of politics, the ideals and principles of parliamentary democracy. Though our practices are based on those of the British House of Commons we are developing our own conventions in response to our distinctive conditions.

You propose to discuss the role of political parties in

legislatures, the relationship of Parliament with Government on the one hand and the people on the other, cabinet government, second chambers, etc., and I hope that your discussions will prove useful.

Democracy is derived from two Greek words meaning people and power. It literally means the rule of the people. We may look at it from different points of view, as a way of life, as a form of government, as an instrument for the development of social and economic content, as a method of approach in the settlement of problems. I shall offer a few general remarks on each of these aspects.

I

The Hebrew prophet said : 'Where there is no vision the people perish.' Democracy gives us a vision, a way of life, asks us to accept certain ideals, norms, or standards of behaviour. The objectives and obligations prescribed in the Preamble and Part IV of the Constitution provide guidance for us.

The dignity of the individual, the sacredness of human personality is the fundamental principle of democracy. There is a tendency to look upon the individual as the helpless victim of world forces which are marching towards their destined goals. The world is becoming anonymous and the individual is getting lost in it. But life is manifested in the individual who learns and suffers, who knows joy and sorrow, forgiveness and hatred. The world owes all its progress to men who are ill at ease. Even the derelicts of humanity, the criminals and the outcasts, each has his Self inside him. The fnuction of the state is to see that the light of human recognition in men's eyes does not grow dim. In a touching poem representing the shy self-encouragement of a lonely young man in a far country, John Masefield writes :

I have seen flowers come in stony places;
And kindness done by men with ugly faces;
And the gold cup by the worst horse at the races;
So I trust too.

If we compromise with the essential freedom of the spirit, all other liberties will disappear.

In the Communist Manifesto, Karl Marx complains about the capitalist order which is, 'for the enormous majority, a mere training to act as a machine. It destroys, he holds, the humanity of the proletriat. The right of the individual to privacy and self-development is one of the cherished rights of democracy.

Apastamba declares: *atmalabhan na param vidyate* (Dharma Sutra, I.7.2) *atmarthe prthvim tyajet.* For the sake of the soul, even the world may be abandoned. What shall it profit a man if he gains the whole world but loses his own soul ?

In these days when the scientific outlook has made historical determinism fashionable, when great men are said to be slaves or instruments of impersonal forces, it is good to stress the role of the individual in history. There is only one safe rule for the historian, said H.A.L. Fisher, that 'we must recognize in the development of human destinies the play of the contingent and the unforeseen.' Inevitability of a demonstration in Euclid does not apply to human affairs. Man has real part in the making of History, *raja kalasya karanam.* While we reject rigid determinism, we cannot represent man as being completely emancipated from the past. The scope of human choice may be limited but it is there, all the same. We are not the playthings of fate. It is not by submerging our identity in the herd but by the creative use of freedom of thought, feeling and imagination, by wresting the initiative from the environment and vesting it in ourselves that we emancipate ourselves from dominion of external forces. If we are able to clothe, feed and house ourselves better, if we are able to release ourselves from want and indignity, it is because of the free spirit of man and its initiative. The whole history of human progress centres round those prophets and heroes, those poets and artists, those pioneers and explorers who dared to take responsibility for their insights into goodness, truth, or beauty, who made their own choices and decisions even at the peril of their lives, for they felt that if they did not do so they would betray the spirit in them. Respect for the individual is the moral basis of a democratic society. In it no one should be a slave and no one a master.

Tocqueville writing about the United States of America

more than a hundred years ago says: "It had been supposed, until our time, that despotism was odious under whatever form it appeared. It is a discovery of modern days that there are such things as legitimate tyranny and holy injustice, provided they are exercised in the name of people." He says: "I know no country in which there is no little true independence of mind and freedom of discussion as in America." Again: "If great writers have not at present existed in America, the reason is very simply given in these facts: there can be no literary genius without freedom of opinion, and freedom of opinion does not exist in America."

II

Jana-vakyam tu kartavyam narair api naradhipaih. The voice of the people must be carried out by the people and the rulers. How are we to ascertain the will of the people ? A mere clamour or catchword is not the will of the people.

Parliamentary democracy seems to be the best instrument for the ascertainment of expression of the public mind. Democracy is government by the representatives chosen by the people. Direct government by the people is not possible in modern States. Even village panchayats adopt the representative system. It gives the people the right to amend and alter the Constitution. So long as it exists, till it is changed by the people's representatives, it is obligatory on all. Unless there is common ground, accepted by all members to whatever party they may belong, the work of Parliament cannot be carried on. Parliamentary democracy provides a peaceful way of changing Government. Frequent elections indicate that people have the power to remove their representatives.

We have adopted universal adult suffrage. This demands universal education. Only then will the voters be able to comprehend national-purpose and duty and use their vote not for selfish ends but for public welfare. Even though our voters are not educated in the formal sense, they have commonsense and an instinctive love of truth and justice.

People are sometimes seduced from these by propagandists and salesmen of new-fanged ideals, class interests, or group loyalties. By exploiting mob psychology people are manipulated, badgered, bribed and hypnotized into different groups. If intelligent nations have tamely submitted to dictatorial governments, it only shows how easily men give up their individual responsibility.

If people are to form sound opinions on social and economic affairs, they must have access to accurate information and an opportunity to hear all sides of the question. The source of information should not be muzzled or controlled by selfish interests. People must have the freedom of thought and expression. In a totalitarian society, the party in power regiments the views of the people through control of all agencies of information, communication and entertainment. All opposition is silenced and people hear only what the Government wants them to hear. It is the function of Parliament to express, not suppress social discontent. In a true democracy, even the thought we hate is tolerated so long as the thought we hold is free to combat it. We should not admit the crime of harbouring dangerous thoughts. Heretics were often liquidated, to use a modern phrase. The Crusades against the Albigensians in Southern France were as barbarous as the Nazi slaughter of the Jews. Only criminals guilty of violence should be restrained. What people think is their own private affair; what they do concerns the public.

Parliament acts as a liaison between the people and the State. It is the place where we sense atmosphere and create it. The leaders do not really merely follow public opinion but lead it. "Your representative," observes Burke in a well-known passage, "owes you not his industry only but his judgment; and he betrays instead of serving you if he sacrifices it to your opinion." If we merely reflect public opinion on the plea that we are concerned with winning votes, then what we say in Parliament will be trite, altitude and demagogy. The decisive consideration should not be whether we do naything popular but whether we do the right. In a majority of cases, when we do wrong we will be unpopular. Terrific pressures discourage acts of political courage.

Members of Parliament should be chosen with care and given training through institutions like your Bureau for Parliamentary Studies. The representative must have an understanding of the Constitution which is the contract between the people and the Government, its directive principles which form our national dharma or righteousness, which is the basis of all rights and duties, which helps to develop the secular and the spiritual interests of the people, *abhpudaya* and *nihshreyasa*.

We have scrapped the dogma of the divine right of kings; even Governments by elected majorities have no divine rights. A democratic government, i.e. government by the majority is open to grave abuses. Lord Action observed: "...that government by the whole people, being the government of the most numerous and most powerful class, is an evil of the same nature as unmixed monarchy, and requires for nearly the same reasons, institutions that shall protect it against arbitrary revolutions of opinion." For a sound democracy we require freedom of thought and expression. This demands respect for minority opinion. In a true democracy there is always an Opposition. It may not be strong in numbers but it does not follow that it is lacking in political intelligence. The Opposition may not compel agreement but it compels thought. Authoritarian methods of suppression of opposition are dangerous to democracy. The Buddha, Socrates and Jesus are symbols. The state can silence them but cannot quench the fire that burns in them. Socrates and Jesus and many others were silenced as grave 'security risks' in the 'cold wars' of their times. Across centuries of despotism and dogma we find the poison cup, the cross, the stake, the torture chamber and the concentration camp. We in India did not liquidate the Buddha or, for that matter, other non-conformists. As a rule we did not confront our people with either conformity or martyrdom. We allowed for freedom which is the way to progress. Nothing has been more disastrous to the world than the common assumption that we are always right. If we suppress those who preach unorthodox ideas and stifle the spirit in man, we are not democratic. What we do with our non-conformists is the test of a democracy.

A Government is not democratic simply because it is voted into power by the majority. It is not democratic when it is required to vote for only one party. The test is whether it gives democratic rights to its subjects, if it allows freedom of thought, speech and association to its opponents. If a party brooks no rivals outside it and no dissensions within it, even if it is voted by the electorate, it is undemocratic.

Part III of our Consitution on Fundamental Rights gives us a set of rights or civil liberties. These rights are the limits which the Government has placed on itself for the protection of the citizens. As even Governments cannot infringe them, we are preserved from tyranny. The highest political good is liberty regulated by just laws. If all men have these rights, they have also a duty to respect the rights of others. Our right ends when it interferes with the right of another. The right to free speech, for example, does not carry the right to an audience, for that interferes with the rights of others.

Democracy means distribution of power, decentralization. An independent Judiciary, Audit and Services Commission restrain Governments from arbitary or tyrannical acts. These institutions require to be protected from the executive interference or political pressure. It is the only way to develop standards of public life, for even the best of men are coarsened and hardened by excess of power. Tyranny becomes habit, nay, a disease. Power should not be centralized.

The aim of society, says Aristotle, is to promote the good life, not the glorification of a Pharaoh or a great emperor. The good life is impossible under the uncalculable caprices of a tyranny; so power should be bridled by law. Aristotle writes: "He who bids law rule bids God and reason alone rule, but he who bids men rule adds the element of the beast." Since no man is fit for unbridled power, commonsense dictates the rule of law. Cicero insists that government is not mere arbitrary power. 'Society is not a mere mob come together anyhow.' He says that it is 'a commonwealth united by acceptance of law and by a common enjoyment of its practical advantages.' Political power is justified only if it advances the common good, *manava dharma*. A tyrant rules by force, a Parliament rules according to law. The great political thinker Edmund Burke said: "Those who give and those who receive arbitrary power are alike criminal and there is no man but is bound to resist it wherever it shows its face in the world. . . . It is wickedness in politics to say that one man can have arbitrary power." We do not want a tyrant or a mob. "The objective of government, according to Spinoza, is not to change men from rational beings into beasts or puppets, but to enable them to develop their reason unshackled." In fact, the true end of government is liberty.

Democratic government rests on clean and efficient administration. The Government is becoming the largest employer with the gradual expansion of the public sector. We must recruit the right type of personnel. Everyone must have an equal chance of securing a Government position and selection should depend on ability, not influence.

III

The democratic approach is by persuasion, argument and adjustment of conflicting views. If there is a difference of opinion, one can say, 'agree with me or I will hit you,' or, 'let us sit down, understand each other and decide.' The latter is the democratic approach. It believes that love is better than hate, cooperation better than strife, consent better than coercion. In the present world to violence is at best a cowardly escape from democratic processes and at worse treason to the future.

There are many problems facing us. To realize freedom of spirit, liberty from physical and social constraints is essential. We can free ourselves from material and social compulsions through right economic ordering of life and the proper fostering of social relationship. Many millions in our country suffer from a slavery far more cruel than chains and shackles. Human-beings are sometimes treated as commodities to be bought and sold. Clauses in the Constitution or laws in the Statute Book are not changes in the structure of society. Poor people who wander about, find no work, no wages and starve, whose lives are a continual round of sore affliction and pinching poverty cannot be proud of the Constitution or its laws. We seem to be poor with the accumulated poverty of centuries. Until we are able to free our citizens from poverty, hunger, disease and ignorance, our democracy will be empty of content. We should achieve a social and economic revolution by methods of persuasion and consent. We believe that we can improve our social environment by argument, conciliation and majority vote. We should have institutions of social conciliation and arbitration. While trade unions are not to be treated as tools of the State, they should not allow sectional interests to prevail over national good. Institutions which have been obstacles to economic well-being and social justice require to be removed. It is true that society should protect itself against crime, for all violence is a menace to the rule of law. But we should also strive to check crime at its source. We must create conditions in which men and women can live and work and face the future with confidence and security.

Democracy is an invitation to a new life. The ideals we have set before ourselves must become fresh. What happened in 1947 is the beginning of a revolution and we have to carry it out. If our Constitution does not bend to the needs of a creative society in which 'the free development of each is the condition for the free development of all', it will break.

Democracy has two sides to it, the making of the individual and the drawing of the world together. A new society is possible only if men prize liberty as the highest of all possessions. We look forward to a new order of society in which the sacredness of personality becomes the working principle, in which the whole world becomes the unit of cooperation, in which every person has equality of opportunity for his complete development, in which there would be a redistribution of the world's economic goods providing equal opportunities for all. The noble vision of a *societas generis humani*, the society of the whole human race is taking shape in the minds of many. If the vision of a creative society, an indivisible democracy weakens, our society will decline. If the idea holds us, we move forward. To establish a creative democracy we should develop the democratic spirit in our hearts. Gandhi taught us that great power resides in the spirit of the people, not in the weapons they use to kill others but in their readiness to die. The Mahabharata says :

naiva rajyam narad aasit na dando na ca dandikah
dharmenaiva prajah sarvah raksanti sma parasparam.

A people flourish not because of a constitution or coercion or a law-giver but because they are guided by dharma and help each other in cooperation.

F. SHRI MORARJI DESAI, EX-PRIME MINISTER OF INDIA

Shri Morarji Desai was not only the ex-Prime Minister of India, he was also a thinker and person of strong will. He is a true follower of Gandhi and has clear views which he puts very logically and impressively whenever there is any opportunity.

He had the rare courage to declare that India shall not manufacture an atomic bomb, though she has successfully exploded one in the past. His speech in the U.N. puts his views and the peaceful policy of Indian Government in a forceful manner.

The following is the text of Mr. Desai's address to the special session of the U.N. Assembly on disarmament :

We have met here at a crucial period of the world's history. Nuclear armament, despite its dangers and threat of extinction to the whole world, has been escalated to a stage when even a small part of its weaponry can destory the whole planet. Conventional arms and the armed forces of the world have attained astronomical proportions and numbers. Even without nuclear armament, we have seen during the last war what amount of destruction the clash of these arms and forces can bring about. We in India believe that this special session of the U.N. General Assembly on disarmament has not met a day too soon and I bring to this august assembly the greetings and good wishes of the peace loving people of India.

Even though the central theme of this session is disarmament, it is also concerned with setting mankind firmly on the path of peace which is also the path of sanity.

I have no doubt, Mr. President, that you will impart to its deliberations the patience, the strength of purpose and the clarity of vision that this momentous task demands. I offer my felicitations to you Mr. President, on being called upon to preside over the session.

Our sages long ago envisaged an ideal which is in the Vedic benediction.

May all people be happy,
May all people be without jealousies,
May all people perceive the good,
May no one get sorrow and misery.

It is this ennobling vision of the world of happiness and contentment which have always borne within me ever since I came in contact with the philosophy and personality of Mahatma Gandhi. It is a vision which we all should cherish and should strive to turn into a reality, not in the distant future, but in our own time.

This presupposes an atmosphere in which, to quote the Biblical saying : "They shall beat their swords into plough shares and their spears into pruning hooks. Nation shall not lift up sword against nation, neither shall they learn war anymore."

The destructive potential of modern weapons used during the Second World War made the world fearful of war and crave for peace. At such a moment of realization was the United Nations founded. Almost simultaneously India achieved freedom through non-violent means under the unique leadership of Mahrtma Gandhi which paved the way for the peaceful liberation of most of the nations from the colonial domination during the last three decades. Viewed against this background and in the context of the near unanimity of world opinion. I believe that the times are propitious, and the prospects of banishing war at present are brighter than at any time before.

It is a sad thought that since times immemorial, the history of societies has always been interspersed with the history of wars. It is even sadder to reflect that, far from being condemned, the warlike attributes of conquering heroes have been exalted and glorified. The literature of every language, and children's books even now, are replete with accounts of human slaughter in battles and wars. Some latter-day conquerors have even tried to seek comfort in the theory of evolution through natural selection and survival of the fittest to provide plausible scientific support to the cult of genocide Refinements of such arguments—racial, material and cultural—are still presented to us with varying degrees of sophistry. War was an accepted instrument of furthering national interests in the past. But it no longer commands the same legitimacy.

The current quest for peace, however, seems to stem from fear of total annihilation. It is my firm conviction that fear is the worst, everlasting and demoralizing influence on man. It should not be the fear of war but love of peace which should rule over actions. International power politics, however, appears to be merely the pursuit of selfish group interests—bringing to surface much that is not noble in man—his pettiness, his suspicion of fellowmen, his jealousies, his greed to acquire and dominate. The result is a general feeling of insecurity and fear leading to culmination in war.

> Peace is not merely cessation of war, but a positive sense of identification with and concern for others. Instead of war, peace must abide in the minds of men. Little good can come of working for peace without a deep conviction that in peace alone there is human fulfilment and happiness. But even if the goal appears distant, it is well worth-striving for because movement in this direction itself reduces the causes of conflict. If we all seek peace, the world will one day become a real human family as embodied in our ancient saying : "The whole world is one family."

In more than 50 years of public life, in office as well as in prison, may I say in all humility that I have been sustained by the conviction, imparted to me by Mahatma Gandhi, that the noblest of ends cannot but be debased by resort to evil means to achieve them. The pursuit of truth with courage and sacrifice—satyagraha—was for Gandhiji not only an article of faith but a guide far practical action. His whole life was a testimoney to the truth that the only real and indeed the ultimate freedom is freedom from fear. This fact has received homage from many, but has also been scoffed at as utopian or unrealistic in the grim world of real-politics. I believe that Gandhiji's message of non-violence and the innovative instrument of satyagraha that he gave us have great relevance in our predicament as we grope for a way out of the present impasse.

If we comprehend the unique and explosive crisis we collectively encounter, we must move towards disarmament through a solemn resolve to outlaw war and settle disputes through the beneficent process of negotiations. Only by doing so would we be true to our charter. So long as war is regarded as legitimate, disarmament will be a himerical Cillusion.

Many wars have been fought in the past because nations were ruled by the desire to acquire power and domination or material goods from others. But after every major human holocaust—whether the European wars of the French revolutionary period or the two World Wars in this century—either because of temporary repentance or exhaustion, there have been attempts to build a structure of peace such as the Congress of Vienna, the League of Nations, or our own United Nations.

Nevertheless, in the working of these institutions, some countries have become involved and have involved others in power politics, in convassing for blocs, competition for spheres of influence, promotion of sales of armaments and piling up of arsenals of terror, conventional and nuclear.

The much-vaunted nuclear deterrent has failed to put an end to the arms race. In fact, it has stimulated further competition, involving vastly destructive weaponry. The delays and difficulties which the Super-Powers have experienced, in coming to an agreement on the test ban—partial or total—on limitation of nuclear armaments, and reduction of the armed strength of NATO and Warsaw Pact countries, over the last 30 years, indicate the utter futility of trying to secure even partial disarmament through a policy of balancing of forces rooted in mutual suspicion and fear.

The commitment to disarmament must therefore be total and without any reservations, although in actual implementation, having regard to the hard realities of the situation, we may accept the principle of gradualness in a time-bound programme, we must keep in view the final objective and, in a spirit of dedication to that objective, work out a non-discriminatory programme based on universal application shorn of any monopolistic feature or preferential treatment.

In this context I should like to refer to the nuclear nonprolification treaty of which much has been said in this hall and outside. India is among those who have not signed this treaty. There has been considerable misunderstanding of our motives. To remove these, I should like to declare that we yield to none in our commitment to comprehensive disarmament.

We are the only country pledged not to manufacture or acquire nuclear weapons even if the rest of the world did so, and I solemnly reiterate that pledge before this august Assembly. In fact we have gone further and abjured nuclear explosion even for peaceful purposes. We ask from others no more than the self-restraint we impose upon ourselves. But our objection to the treaty is because it is so potently discriminatory. It makes an invidious distinction between countries having nuclear weaponry and those devoted to the pursuit of nuclear research and technology entirely for peaceful purposes. Paradoxically, the treaty gives the former a monopoly of power and confers on them freedom for commercial exploitation of nuclear know-how, while on the latter it places restrictions which may impede peaceful development of nuclear science. Along with the partial test ban treaty, the NPT has placed the nuclear military Powers in a position which enables them to continue with the utilization of nuclear energy for military purpose while telling others' "thus far and no further."

Despite protestations of peace and despite realization of the dangers of nuclear warfare, the Super-Powers between them have conducted 254 nuclear tests during the last eight years. The NPT has thus failed to arrest the growth of nuclear armaments either qualitatively or quantitatively as anticipated. The weapons now with the Super-Powers are deadlier and larger in numbers.

The history of the deliberations of this Assembly and of the various committees particularly the conference of the committee on disarmament, shows that even though the two co-chairmen, the USSR and USA, have been active between themselves and with others and in the various committees, they have yet to provide a basis on which general agreements on the several aspects of disarmament could be reached.

I am sure they recognize this and it is the general view that the onus for finding the solution of the problems connected with nuclear disarmament lies heavily on them. In the discharge of that responsibility, suspicion and fear can have no place. This is not a matter of ideology or of narrow national interests, but of an assurance against the tragedy that the erosion of such a trust may entail and which may engulf the whole world. It is in this sense that we regard nuclear armament as a threat to the very survival of humanity.

I am glad that the distinguished Presidents of the USA and the USSR recognize the urgency of finding a solution. The distinguished Presidents of the USA and USSR have expressed their determination to finalize expeditiously the negotiations for the elimination of the testing of all nuclear devices, whether for development or military purposes, and for the SALT-II agreement.

Certain other agreements, as for instance the banning of radiological weapons are in the offing. From here; President Carter has solemnly declared last year that the United States will not use nuclear weapons except in self-defence. I am also happy that President Brezhnev has spoken of the replacement of balance of terror by the balance of trust. While these are welcome signs holding out some hope for the future, we have yet to see these benevolent intentions translated into action. I share the concern of the distinguished President of France over the delays in these negotiations and the limited nature of the deliberations on disarmament which have preceded the convening of this conference.

My own earnest submission to this Assembly is that the problem of disarmament, particularly in the nuclear field, cannot be solved by a system of cheeks end balances devised as a result of bargaining. It can only be solved in a total manner, keeping in view the whole of the globe end not the regions into which, presumably as a matter of political convenience or strategy. Some countries seek to compartmentalize the word. It is idle to talk of regional nuclear-free zones when there would still be zones which could continue to be endangered by nuclear weapons. Those who have such weapons lose nothing if some distant area is declared non-nuclear. The nations without nuclear capacity who imagine that their inclusion in such zones affords them security are suffering from a delusion. We are convinced that there cannot be a united approach to the question of freedom from nuclear threats and dangers, but the whole world should be declared as a nuclear free zone.

It is now widely recognized that we have given sufficient time to the policies based on violence to work out a system of peace and security and that we have now reached a point of expansion. We have therefore to take decisive steps to turn the minds of nations away from violence as an insurance of safety and security, and take them towards non-violence and satyagraha as means of resisting wrong.

Although I have urged and will continue to urge that the ultimate solution lies in the general acceptance of the philosophy and practice of non-violence. I believe with Gandhiji that one step is enough for me to start with but that step must mean abjuring of violence as an instrument and a substantial reduction in the weapons and instruments of violence.

> That first step in my view must consist of : (a) a declaration that utilization of nuclear technology for military purposes, including research in weapon technology must be outlawed; (b) qualitative and quantitatiue limitations on nuclear armament and immediate freezing of the present stockpile under international inspection; (c) formulation of a time-bound programme—not exceeding a decade—for gradual reduction of the stockpile with a view to achieving total elimination of all nuclear weapons; and (d) a comprehensive test ban treaty with provision for safeguards to prevent breach of the treaty which in my view can only be through independent inspection.

The ban should apply to atmospheric, underground and undersea tests and those in space. I would also add that the system of safeguards should be based on universality and non-discrimination. We must ensure that the system of inspection and safeguards is enforced objectively and without bringing politics into such enforcement.

For initating a programme of disarmament in the conventional field. We would not wait until nuclear disarmament is completed. We should this very year begin efforts to work out an agreement on disarmament and drastic reduction in the armed strength in the conventional field. I can assure this Assembly on behalf of my country the India will cooperate to the fullest extent in the formulation of these various programmes and will pledge it to their implementation.

In fact, we should visualize a time when the use of armed forces would not be necessary, even for internal security.

Mr. President, the resources of the world we live in are too precious to be wasted on destruction. Millions round the globe suffer from want, from malnutrition, from under-development and from a despair about today and tomorrow. We have misused the world's wealth for far too long. Let us now resolve to harness science and statesmanship to the cause of the happiness of mankind. Let us send out from here a message of succour and relief to the poor, the infirm, the under-nourished and enable them to draw an assurance that a better life a better world will be theirs.

It would be too much to claim that the eyes of all those people are on our Assembly here. For many of them are unlettered and preoccupied with the exacting task of earning their daily bread. Then the literate citizens of the advanced countries are not in a position to restrain their Government. But they do know that all their comfort and affluence will be wiped out if some one presses a button somewhere. This apprehension is one of the basic causes of the anguish which makes life recariouslyun certain in affluent countries, especially amongst the young. All this adds to the responsibility of all of us.

It should be clear to us all that no scheme of global peace and disarmament can last unless it is linked with the creation of an equitable world economic order. The nuclear Powers and their close allies are also those who dominate the world's economy and manage it to their own advantage. Their military and economic strength reinforce each other. The poorer countries have to face not only the threat of domination but also the denial of fair return for their produce and their labour. Disarmament could and should serve the larger purpose of correlating the economic injustice and deprivation to which two-thirds of humanity is subject today.

Even if a small portion of the $ 1 billion a day that are now spent on armaments could be diverted to the benevolent service of mankind through the spread of irrigation, the feeding of the undernourished, to educating the unlettered, to curing and ministering the sick and the infirm in all countries, to purifying the world's air and water, and to enlarging the understanding of other people's cultures, it would bring the ideal of a brave new world nearer achievement.

I suggest that this Assembly recommend the setting up of a fund which would carry out studies in disarmament and non-violence and find out ways and means of replacing bombs and bullets by bread and books.

Working for abolition of war is not only a historical necessity, but a human duty. It is a plain matter of enlightened self-interest since it is indissolubly linked without very survival.

If all this power of destruction came from the human intellect, surely that same intellect can create something more compassionate and benevolent. The old prophets and seers who laid the foundations of human civilization may not have seen the mushroom clouds of atomic bombs. But they knew the nature of power, with their capacity to see the whole tree within the tiny seed. In one of our ancient books—the Kathopanshadi—there is a parable of a boy of tender years who carries on a dialogue with the God of Death who is also the God of Justice. The God offers the boy all the riches, all the pleasures and all the glory there can be. But Nachiketa, the boy, wants to know the nature of life, and death and immortality. God parts with the mystery, but like all mysteries, it is not so mysterious.

Victory over death, he says, comes from self-control. Likening the body to a chariot, the mind to reins, the senses to horses, and the objects of the senses to the roads, he adds: He who has no understanding and whose mind is never firmly held his senses are unmanageable, like vicious horses of a chariot. But he who has understanding and whose mind is always firmly held, his senses are under control like good horses of a chariot.

What is true of the individual is true of the world community. Man who has invented these engines of destruction is also filled with a desire for immortality. At this moment, death and life are poised as on a razor's edge. Let us choose life. It is for this Assembly, representing the collective wisdom of mankind, to launch a movement in the conscience of men and embark on the great adventure of survival with determination not to compromise with truth.

CHAPTER 4

WESTERN THOUGHTS FROM VOLTAIRE TO KANT

A. VOLTAIRE

The original name of Voltaire was Francois Marie Arouet. He was born on November 21,1694 in Paris. His father was a lawyer. From the very beginning he had weak health. But despite this weak health, he not only lived for eighty long years; he led an extremely jestful and struggleful life.

His father naturally wanted to make his son a lawyer like himself. But his gifted son would not accept the plan of his father. He wanted to become an ambassador's page. With this intention he left France and went to Holland. It is said that there he tried to carry off his beloved and because of his wanton act, he was sent back to France.

Voltaire was not a person who would sit quietly. He wrote against the cruelties of the then despotic French Government and therefore was sent to the Bastille. He remained behind the bars for one year but kept himself quite busy with writing work. He composed poems and tragedies which made him famous.

He was merely thirty at that time. Because of his money and fame, Voltaire led a very romantic life. This brought him into clash with a noble man of his time named Chevalier de Rohan-Chabot. And as the latter was an influential person, Voltaire again found himself within the walls of the Bastille. But this incident made Voltaire bitter against society which tolerates injustice.

Voltaire went to England after his release. The free atmosphere of English life impressed him. He was deeply influenced by Locke, Swift, and Newton.

He returned to France in 1729 and found himself surrounded by fame and prosperity due to his writings. But Voltaire had become very sober due to his past experiences and wrote a very thoughtful work Letters *Philosophiques sur les Anglais* wherein he described the English institutions. He demanded civil and religious freedom for his people. The Government naturally proscribed the work and the work was burned in the court of the Palais de justice. Voltaire himself fled away to escape punishment.

Voltaire's lady admirer and friend Marquise du Chatelet helped him in this plight. But when she befriended another gentleman, Voltaire fled to the King of Prussia, Frederick II. From there he went to Switzerland. But everywhere fanatics chased him. Voltaire very wisely built two houses on the borders of France and Switzerland. They were very close. The moment he would be hunted out in one, he would go to the other. He wrote: "Thus crawling from one lair to the other, I escape from kings and armies."

Voltaire fought against tyranny and injustice. His was a dauntless spirit which was not afraid of opposing anybody. The poor and the helpless who were victims of cruelty and injustice would come to him, and Voltaire would fight for them. This fearless fight for getting justice for the countless people made him very famous. Voltaire's merit lies in his ceaseless fight against forces of ignorance, blind orthodoxy, and injustice. In the domain of religion he exposed the elements of cheating and deceit and fraud. Voltaire himself believed in the existence of God. He wrote: "Belief in a God who rewards good deeds and punishes bad ones is the belief most useful to mankind. It is the only curb on powerful men; it is the only curb on men who skilfully commit secret crimes. Fifteenth-century Italy swarmed with atheists. What happend ? It was as common to poison a man as to give him supper, and to sink a stiletto in your friend's heart as to embrace him... I do not ask you to mingle with this necessary faith the superstitions which dishonour it. The atheist is a monster: the victim of superstition is another monster... the narrow zone of virtue lies between atheism and fanaticism. Belief in a good God, and be good... I should hate to deal with an atheist prince who found it to his interest to have me pounded in a mortar; I am very sure that I should be pounded. If I were a sovereign I should hate to deal with atheist courtiers. It is necessary to princes and peoples that the idea of a Supreme Being should be deeply engraved in their minds..." To Voltaire belongs the credit of being the first philosopher of history. He was inspired for undertaking this task by Mme. du Chatrlet who had told him: "What does it matter to me, a French woman living on my estate, to know that Egil succeeded Haquin in Sweden, and that Ottoman was the son of Ortogrul... I renounce a study that overwhelms the mind without illuminating it." The rational mind of Votaire grasped the point immediately. His Ingenu says: "History is nothing more than a picture of crimes and misfortunes." He himself wrote to Horace Walpole on July 15, 1768; "Truly the history of the Yorkists and the Lancastrians, and many other, is much like reading the history of highway robbers." Disgusted with such accounts of history, he had declared "Only philosophers should write history" Hence, he decided to write history in his own way. He unfolded his plan by stating : "I wish to write a history not of wars, but of society ; and to ascertain how men lived in the interior of their families, and what were the arts which they commonly cultivated...My object is the history of the human mind, and not a mere detail of pretty facts; nor am I concerned with the history of great lords...; but I want to know what were the steps by which men passed from barbarism to civilization." Its title was Essay on the Morals and the Spirit of the Nations from Charlemagne to Louis XIII. The Conclusion that he drew from such a philosophical study of history was very illuminating; "From this picture we see that everything belonging intimately to human nature is alike from one end of the universe to the other, while everything depending on custom is different. Custom produces variety; nature unity. The soil is everywhere the same, and cultivation produces different fruits."

The only objective behind the profuse writings of Voltaire was to arouse human rationality so that misdeeds of folly may be eradicated. For example, in his work "Micromegas", which is, to certain extent, an imitation of Swift, the earth is visited by an inhabitant from Sirius; he is some 500,000 feet tall. In that work Sirian declares: "O ye intelligent atoms, in whom the Supreme Being hath been pleased to manifest his omniscience and power, without doubt your joys on this earth must be pure and exquisite; for being unencumbered with matter, and—to all appearance—little else than soul, you must spend your lives in the delights of pleasure and reflection, which are the true enjoyments of a perfect spirit. True happiness I have nowhere found; but certainly here it dwells"

"We have matter enough," answered one of the philosophers, "to do abundance of mischief....You must know, for example, that at this very moment, while I am speaking, there are 100,000 animals of our own species, covered with hats, slaying an equal number of their follow creatures, who wear turbans; at least they are either slaying or being slain; and this has usually been the case all over the earth from time immemorial."

"Miscreants", cried the indignant Sirian, "I have a good mind to take two or three steps, and trample the whole nest of such ridiculous assassins under my feet."

"Don't give yourself the trouble," replied the philosopher, "they are industrious enough in securing their own destruction. At the end of ten years the hundredth part of these wretches will not survive...Besides, the punishment should not be inflicted upon them, but upon those sedentry and slothful barbarians who, from their places, give orders for murdering a million men, and then solemnly thank God for their successes".

This aecount from his Micromegas, thus clearly proves how bitterly Voltaire felt about the failings of humanity.

In the same spirit Voltaire's Zadig contains a piercing attack on human irrationality :

"He (Zadig) then represented to himself the human species, as it really is, as a parcel of insects devouring one another on a little atom of clay. This true image seemed to annihilate his misfortunes, by making him sensible of the nothingness of his own being and that of Babylon. His soul launched into infinity; and detached from the Senses, contemplated the immutable order of the universe." Voltaire was a pacifist and considered war as foolish. He condemned the Seven Years' War that was fought between England and France for the possession of Canada. He considered the war as madness and suicide. It was foolish to fight for "a few acres of snow". The sole object of Voltaire was to stir up human constructive thought. For example his most famous work "Candide" contains the following conversation between Candide, a simple and honest lad, and an old sage, Martin.

"Do you believe," said Candide, "that men have always massacred one another as they do today , that they have always been liars, cheats, traitors, ingrates, brigands, idiots, thieves, scoundrels, gluttons, drunkards, misers, envious, ambitious, bloody-minded, calumniators, debauchees, fanatics, hypocrites and fools ?"

"Do you believe," said Martin, "that hawks have always eaten pigeons when they have found them ?"

"Without doubt, ' said Candide.

"Well, then," said Martin, "if hawks have always had the same character why should you imagine that men have changed theirs ?"

"Oh", said Candide, "there is a vast deal of difference, for free will."

One of the most notable works of Voltaire is his Philosophic Dictionary. The Dictionary contains Voltaire's thoughts about various subjects arranged alphabetically.

Voltaire was convinced that war is madness. "War is the greatest of all crimes; and yet there is no aggressor who does not colour his crime with the pretext of justice." wrote Voltaire. And he very correctly added "It is forbidden to kill;

therefore all murderers are punished unless they kill in large numbers and to the sound of trumpets."

Writing under the head of "man" in the Dictionary he very reflectively stated :

"Twenty years are required to bring man from the state of a plant, in which he exists in the womb of his mother, and from the state of an animal, which is his condition in infancy, to a state in which the maturity of reason begins to make itself felt. Thirty centuries are necessary in which to discover even a little of his structure. An eternity would be required to know anything of his soul. But one moment suffices in which to kill him."

It is really very refreshing to go through the constructive thoughts of Voltaire in our age when human being has turned himself into a terrible monster and has put the very earth into the danger of utter destruction.

ESSENCE OF VOLTAIRE'S THOUGHT FROM PHILOSOPHIC DICTIONARY

Man (Is Man Born Wicked ?)

Is it not demonstrated that man is not born perverse and the child of the devil ? If such was his nature, he would commit enormous crimes and barbarities as soon as he could walk; he would use the first knife he could find, to wound whoever displeased him. He would necessarily resemble little wolves and foxes, who bite as soon as they can. On the contrary, throughout the world, he partakes of the nature of the lamb, while he is an infant. Why, therefore, and how is it that he so often becomes a Wolf and fox ? It is not that, being born neither good nor wicked, education, example, the government into which he is thrown—in short occasion of every kind—determines him to virtue or vice ? Perhaps human nature could not be otherwise. Man could not always have false thoughts, nor always true affections; be always sweet, or always cruel.

It is demonstrable that woman is elevated beyond men in the scale of goodness. We see a hundred brothers enemies to each other, to one Clytemnestra.

There are professions which necessarily render the soul pityless—those of the soldier, the butcher, the officer of justice, and the jailor; and all trades which are founded on the annoyance of others.

Whoever has been able to descend to the subaltern detail of the bar: whoever has only heard lawyers reason familiarly among themselves, and applaud themselves for the miseries of their clients, must have a very poor opinion of human nature.

Women, incessantly occupied with the education of their children, are everwhere less barbarous than men.

Physics join with morals to prevent them from great crimes; their blood is milder; they are less addicted to strong liquors, which inspire ferocity. An evident proof is, that of thousand victims of justice in a thousand executed assassins, we scarcely reckon four women. It is also proved elsewhere, I believe, that in Asia there are not two examples of wowen condemned to a public punishment. It appears, therefore, that our customs and habits have rendered the male species very wicked. If this truth was general and without exceptions, the species would be more horrible than spiders, wolves and polecats are to our eyes. But happily, professions which harden the heart and fill it with odious passions, are very rare. Observe, that in a nation of twenty millions, there are at most two hundred thousand soldiers. This is but one soldier to two hundred individuals.

The number of other trades which are dangerous to manners, is but small. Labourers, artisans, and artists are too much occupied often to deliver themselves up to crime. The earth will always bear detestable wretches, and books will always exaggerate the number, which, rather than being greater, is less than we say.

If mankind had been under the empire of the devil, there would be no longer any person upon earth. Let us console ourselves : we have seen, and we shall always see, fine minds from Pekin to La Rochelle; and whatever licentiates and bachelors may say, the Tituses, Trojans, Antoninuses, and Peter Bayles were very honest men.

GENERAL REFLECTION OF MAN

"It needs twenty years to lead man from the plant state in which he is with in his mother's womb, and the pure animal state which is the lot of his early childhood, to the state when the maturity of the reason begins to appear. It has needed thirty centuries to learn a little about his structure. It would need eternity to learn something about his soul. It takes an instant to kill him."

Voltaire's Philosophical Dictionary.

FATHERLAND

A young journeyman pastrycook who had been to college, and who still knew a few of Cicero's phrases. boasted one day of loving his fatherland' "What do you mean by your fatherland ?" a neighbour asked him. "Is it your oven? is it the village where you were born and which you have never seen since? is it the street where dwelled your father and mother who have been ruined and have reduced you to baking little pies for a living?is it the townhall where you will never be police superintendent's clerk? is it the church of our Lady where you have not been able to become a choir-boy, while an absurd man is archbishop and duke with an income of twenty thousand golden louis?"

The journeyman pastrycook did not know what to answer. A thinker who was listening to this conversation, concluded that in a fatherland of some extent there were often many thousand men who had no fatherland. You, pleasure loving Parisian, who have never made any great journey save that to Dieppe to eat fresh fish; who know nothing but your vanished town house, your pretty country house, and your box at that Opera where the rest of Europe persists in feeling bored;who speak your own language agreeably enough because you know no other, you love all that, and you love further the girls you keep, the champagne which comes to you from Rheims, the dividends which the Hotel-de-ville pays you every six months, and you say you love your fatherland. In all conscience, does a financier cordially love his fatherland? The officer and the soldier who will pillage their winter quarters, if one lets them, have they a very warm love for the peasants they ruin?

Where was the fatherland of the scarred Duc de Guise, was it in Nancy, Paris, Madrid, Rome?

What fatherland have you, Cardinals de La Balue, Duprat, Lorraine, Mazarin?

Where was the fatherland of Attila and of a hundred heroes of this type?

I would like someone to tell me which was Abraham's father land.

The first man to write that the fatherland is wherever one feels comfortable was, I believe, Euripides in his "Phaeton". But the first man who left his birthplace to seek his comfort elsewhere had said it before him.

Where then is the fatherland? Is it not a good field, whose owner, lodged in well-kept house, can say: "This field that I till, this house that I have built, are mine; I live there protected by laws which no tyrant can infringe. When those who, like me, possess fields and houses meet in their common interest, I have my voice in the assembly; I an a part of everything, a part of the cmmunity, a part of the dominion; there is my fatherland?."

Well now, is it better for your fatherland to be a monarchy or a republic? For four thousnd years has this question be debated. Ask the rich for an answer, they all prefer aristocracy; question the people, they want democracy; only kings prefer royalty. How then is it that nearly the whole world is governed by monarchs? Ask the rats who proposed to hang a bell round the cat's neck. But in truth, the real reason is, as has been said, that men are very rarely worthy of governing themselves. It is sad that often in order to be a good patriot one is the enemy of the rest of mankind. To be a good patriot is to wish that one's city may be enriched by trade, and be powerful by arms. It is clear one country cannot gain without another loses, and that it cannot conquer without making misery. Such then is the human state that to wish for one's scountry's greatness is to wish harm to one's neighbours. He who should wish that this fatherland might never be greater, smaller, richer, poorer, would be the citizen of the world.

Voltaire's Philosophical Dictionary

B. IMMANUEL KANT

Kant occupies a place in the galaxy of outstanding thinkers of the world.His contribution to the philosophical thought has been not only noteworthy, it influenced a number of subsequent thinkers like Hegel, Schopenhaur, Marx, Bergson, William James, Sartre etc. in some way or the other.

Kant was born in 1724 and died in the year 1804. It is interesting to note that this thinker practically never left his city, though his philosophy sought to discover the truth of the world,His mother influenced him much. She was a pietist and strictly followed her religious observations. It appears that child Kant also emulated his mother. The result was that in his adult life he kept himself away from the official church but at the same time led a very puritanic life. German poet Heinrich has observed about Kant:

"...he had neither life nor history, for he lived a mechanically ordered and abstract old bachelor life in a quiet retired street in Koenigsberg, an old town on the northeast border of Germany." And he further adds: "I do not believe that the great clock of the cathedral there did its daily work more dispassionately and regularly than its compatriot Immanuel Kant. Rising, coffee drinking, writing, reading college lectures, eating walking, all had their fixed time,and the neighbours knew that it was exactly half past three when Immanuel Kant......left his house door and went to the Lime Tree Avenue, which is still called, in memory of him, the philosopher's Walk."

Kant was thus very regular in life and conduct. It is said that he used to rise at five in the morning and used to go to bed at 10 in night daily There was no break to this daily rule. Kant remained bachelor because of his habit of adopting lengthy deliberation about everything. Fate sent him two opportunities to marry. But in both the cases he could not avail of them. In the first case, Kant's deliberation was so lengthy that the lady preferred to marry another gentleman; in the second Kant's deliberation lasted for such a long time that lady left the town itself before his deliberation was over.

Kant was employed in the University of Konigsbers. But his income was not sufficient. He had to undertake private tutions to make good the deficit. Kant always liked to teach to the persons of average intelligence because he thought that the genius does not need any coaching and the stupid cannot avail of teaching. As can be expected, Kant was a sincere and competent teacher. Many of his pupils shone in later life. Kant was primarily influenced by two thinkers, viz. Rousseau and Hume. The former gave him this idea that he had some duty towards mankind, while the latter taught him to think in the light of strict logic. He has frankly admitted the debt of both these thinkers. For example, he writes about Rousseau:

"I am myself by inclination a seeker after truth. I feel a consuming thirst for knowledge and a restless passion to advance it. There was a time when I thought that this alone could constitute the honour of mankind, and I despised the common man who knows nothing, Rousseau set me right... I learned to respect human nature, and I should consider myself far more useless than the ordinary workingman if did not believe that this view could give worth to all others to establish the rights of man." And about David Hume Kant wrote that he woke him up from his dogmatic slumbers.

But Kant had an original mind. His first work "Theory of Heavens," which was concerned with physics, put forth the nebular hypothesis to explain the origin of the earth. It appears that some forty years later Laplace who is credited with theory, was inspired by Kant.Similarly, Kant's other work "Anthropology" (published in 1798)suggested that human being probably descended from the beast because had human child cried at the birth as it cries at present, it would have been devoured by the beast. Therefore it is possible that humanbeing was different from what he is at present. "How nature brought about such a development, and by what causes it was aided, we know not. This remark carries us a long way. It suggests the thought whether the present period of history,on the occasion of some great physical revolution, may not be followed by a third, when an orangeoutang or a chimpanzee would develop the organs which serve for walkiing, touching, speaking, into the articulated structure of a human being, with a central organ for the use of understanding, and gradually advance under the training of social institutions."

But Kant's most famous work is "Critique of Pure Reason". It was published in 1781. Kant was sure that his work did immense service to the world of knowledge. He wrote: "In this book I have chiefly aimed at completeness; and I venture to maintain that there ought not to be one single metaphysical problem that has not deen solved here, or to the solution of which the key at least has not been supplied."

Kant established in the work that human mind is not a *tabula rasa* or a passive clean slate on which experience is written.

"Experience is by no means the only field to which our understanding can be confined. Experience tells us what is, but not that it must be necessarily what it is and not otherwise. It therefore never gives us any really general truths; and our reason, which is particularly anxious for that class of knowledge, is roused by it rather than satisfied. General truths, which at the same time, bear the character of an inward necessity, must be independent of experience—clear and certain in themselves."

Kant's contention was that "a priori intuitions and concepts" function as containers of man's sensory perceptions. Then the sensory impressions are related and given the shape of coherent thought. Mind plays the role of synthesiser of our experience. Kant further delared that human mind cannot know the "things-in-themselves" or "noumena". It can only know the phenomena, i.e. things as they appear before us.

Kant's other works "Groundwork of the Metaphysic of Morals" and "Critique of Practical Reason" are similarly im-tant, though for other reasons. While in his Critique of Pure Reason Kant concluded that from the point of reason existence of even God cannot be proved, in his works of ethics he tried to prove the existence of God on moral grounds.

Kant put forth four fundamental categorical imperatives in his theory of ethics, viz.

(i) Act only on that principle which you can at the same time will to become a universal law.

(ii) So act as to treat humanity, both in your own person and in the person of every other, always at the same time as an end, never simply as means.

(iii) Act as a member of kingdom of ends.

(iv) A principle of moral conduct is morally binding on me if and only if I can regard it as a law which I impose on myself.

The substance of Kant's ethical philosophy was that a human being is free and he should respect the freedom of all his fellow human beings.

In this respect Kant was definitely influenced by Rousseau.

At the age of sixty-nine, Kant wrote "Religion within the Limits of Pure Reason" which bears the stamp of his independent thinking and perhaps also shows that he was influenced by Voltaire. In this work Kant established that Christ's religion has been deformed and deprived by the official Church. He wrote : "Christ has brought the kingdom of God nearer to earth; but he has been misunderstood; and in place of God's kingdom the kingdom of the priest has been established among us." He added that many types of "pious nonsense" are inculcated as a sort of "heavenly court service by means of which one may win through flattery the favour of the ruler of heaven."

It can be easily judged from all this that Kant was a very liberal thinker. His rational mind persuaded him to discard everything that was irrational. Kant had humanitarian spirit. He even welcomed the French Revolution which came when Kant was sixty-five. He is said to have told his friends with tears of joy : "Now I can say like Simeon, 'Lord, let now Thy servant depart in peace; for mine eyes have seen Thy salvation." In 1784 Kant even wrote "The Natural Principle of the Political Order considered in connection with the Idea of a Universal Cosmopolitical History." Kant established in this work that the element of struggle found in man is essential for his progress. He wrote: "Without qualities of an unsocial kind......men might have led an Arcadian shepherd life in complete harmony, contentment, and mutual love; but in that case all their talents would have forever remained hidden in their germ."

Kant however thought humanity is slowly but steadily moving towards one World State. He stated: "The history of the human race, viewed as a whole, may be regarded as the realization of a hidden plan of nature to bring about a political constitution, internally and externally perfect as the only state in which all the capacities implanted by her in mankind can be fully developed."

Kant's other work "Eternal Peace" was published in 1795 when he was seventy-one. In this work Kant showed how peace can be established on earth. He was of the opinion that so long as armies shall remain, conflicts shall continue. Wars are begun because nations want to plunder other nations. He suggested that to end the cult of war let us decide that war shall be declared only "by a plebiscite of all the citizens." Kant's opinion on the ways of ending wars has importance even in our own period because our world is facing the grimmest possible specture of destruction.

PERPETUAL PEACE

Whether this satirical inscription on a Dutch innkeeper's sign upon which a burial ground was painted had for its object mankind in general, or the rulers of states in particular, who are insatiable of war, or merely the philosophers who dream this sweet dream, it is for us to decide. But one condition the author of this essay wishes to lay down. The practical politician assumes the attitude of looking down with great self-satisfaction on the political theorist as a pedant whose empty ideas in no way threaten the security of the state inasmuch as the state must proceed on empirical principles; so the theorist is allowed to play his game without interference from the worldly-wise statesman. Such being his attitude, the practical politician—and this is the condition I make—should at least act consistently in the case of a conflict and not suspect some danger to the state in the political theorist's opinions which are ventured and publicly expressed without any ulterior purpose. By this clausula salvatoria the author desires formally and emphatically to deprecate herewith any malevolent interpretation which might be placed on his words.

Section I

Containing the preliminary articles for perpetual peace among States.

1 "No Treaty of Peace shall Be Held Valid in Which There Is Tacitly Reserved Matter for a Future War."

....

2 "No Independent States, Large or small, shall Come under the Dominion of Another State by Inheritance, Exchange, Purchase, or Donation."

....

3 "Standing Armies (miles perpetus) Shall in Time Be Totally Abolished."

For they incessantly menace other states by their readiness to appear at all times prepared for war; they incite them to compete with each other in the number of armed men, and there is no limit to this. For this reason, the cost of peace finally becomes more oppressive than that of a short war, and consequently a standing army is itself a cause of offensive war waged in order to relieve the State of this burden. Add to this that to pay men to kill or to be killed seems to entail using them as mere machines and tools in the hands of another (the state), and this is hardly compatible with the rights of mankind in our own person. But the periodic and voluntary military exercises of citizens who thereby secure themselves and the country against foreign aggression are entirely different.

The accumulation of treasure would have the same effect, for, of the three powers—the power of armies, of alliances, and of money—the third is perhaps the most dependable weapon. Such accumulation of treasure is regarded by other states as a threat of war, and if it were not for the difficulties in learning the amount, it would force the other to make an early attack.

4 "National Debts Shall Not Be Contracted with a View to the External Friction of States."

....

5 "No State shall by Force Interfere with the Constitution or Government of Another State."

....

6 "No State Shall, during War, Permit Such Acts of Hostility Which Would Make Mutual Confidence in the Subsequent Peace Impossible : Such Are the Employment of Assassins (percussors), Poisoners (venefici), Breach of Capitulation, and Incitement to Treason (perduellio) in the Opposing State."

Section II

Containing the definitive articles for perpetual peace among states.

The state of peace among men living side by side is not the natural state; the natural state is one of war. This does not always mean open hostilities, but at least unceasing threat of war. A state of peace, therefore, must be established, for in order to be secured against hostility it is not sufficient that hostilities simply be not committed and, unless this security is pledged to each by his neighbour (a thing that can occur only in a civil state), each may treat his neighbour, from whom he demands this security, as an enemy.

First Definitive Article for Perpetual Peace

"The Civil Constitution of Every state should be Republican."

....

To conform to the concept of law, however, government must have a representative form, and in this system only a republican mode of government is possible; without it, government is despotic and arbitrary, whatever the constitution may be..................

Second Definitive Article for a Perpetual Peace

"The Law of Nations shall be Founded on a Federation of Free States"

....

For these reasons there must be a league of a particular kind, which can be called a league of peace, and which would be distinguished from a treaty of peace by the fact that the latter terminates only one war while the former seeks to make an end of all wars forever. This league does not tend to any domination over the power of the state but only to the maintenance and security of the freedom of the state itself and of other states in league with it, without there being any need for them to submit to civil laws and their compulsion, as men in a state of nature must submit.

The practicability (objective reality) of this idea of federation, which should gradually spread to all states and thus lead to perpetual peace, can be proved. For if fortune directs that a powerful and enlightened people can make itself a republic. which by its nature must be inclined to perpetual peace, this gives a fulcrum to the federation with other states so that they may adhere to it and thus secure freedom under the idea of the law of nations. By more and more such associations, the federation may be gradually extended.........The concept of a law of nations as a right to make war does not really mean anything, because it is then a law of deciding what is right by unilateral maxims through force and not by universally valid public laws which restrict the freedom of each one. The only conceivable meaning of such a law of nations might be that it serves men right who are so inclined that they should destroy each other and thus find perpetual peace in the vast grave that swallows both the atrocities and their perpetrators. For states in their relation to each other, there cannot be any reasonable way out of the lawless condition which entails only war except that they, like individual men, should give up their savage (lawless) freedom, adjust themselves to the constraints of public law, and thus establish a continuously growing state consisting of various nations, which will ultimately include all the nations of the world. But under the idea of the law of nations they do not wish this, and reject in practice what is correct in theory. If all is not to be lost, there can be, then, in place of the positive idea of a world republic, only the negative surrogate of an alliance which averts war, endures, spreads, and holds back the stream of those hostile passions which fear the law, though such an alliance is in constant peril of their breaking loose again.

Third definite article for a Perpetual Peace

"The Law of World Citizenship shall be Limited to Conditions of Universal Hospitability."

.........Hospitability means the right of a stranger not to be treated as an enemy when he arrives in the land of another...... Since the narrower or wider community of the peoples of the earth has developed so far that a violation of rights in one place is felt throughout the world, the idea of a law of world citizenship is no high-flown or exaggerated notion. It is a supplement to the un-written code of the civil and international law, indispensable for maintenance of the public human rights and hence also of perpetual peace. One cannot flatter oneself into believing one can approach this peace except under the condition outlined here.

First Supplement

Of the guarantee for Perpetual Peace

The guarantee of perpetual peace is nothing less than that great artist, nature. In her mechanical course we see that her aim is to produce a harmony among men, against their will and indeed through their discord. As a necessity working according to laws we do not know, we call it destiny. But, considering its design in world history, we call it 'providence', inasmuch as we discern in it the profound wisdom of a higher cause which predetermines the course of nature and directs it to the objective final end of the human race. We do not observe or infer this providence in the cunning contrivances of nature, but, as in question of the relation of the form of things to ends in general, we can and must supply it from our own minds in order to conceive of its possibility by analogy to actions of human art. The idea of the relationship and harmony between these actions and the end which reason directly assigns to us is transcendent from a theoretical point of view; from a practical standpoint, with respect, for example, to the ideal of perpetual peace, the concept is dogmatic and its reality is well established, and thus the mechanism of nature may be employed to that end. The use of the word 'nature' is more fitting to the limits of human reason and more modest than an expression indicating a providence unknown to us. This is especially true when we are dealing with questions of theory and not of religion, as at present, for human reason in questions of the relation of effects to their causes must remain within the limits of possible experience. On the other hand, the use of the word 'providence' here intimates the possession of wings like those of Icarus, conducting us toward the secret of its unfathomable purpose.

Before we more narrowly define the guarantee which nature gives, it is necessary to examine the situation in which she has placed her actors on her vast stage, a situation which finally assures peace among them. Then we shall see how she accomplishes the latter. Her preparatory arrangements are :

1. In every region of the world she has made it possible for men to live.
2. By war she has driven them even into the most inhospitable regions in order to populate them.
3. By the same means, she has forced them into more or less lawful relations with each other.

That in the cold wastes by the Arctic Ocean the moss grows which the reindeer digs from the show in order to make itself the prey or the conveyance of the Ostyak or Samoyed; or that the saline sandy deserts are inhabited by the camel which appears created as it were in order that they might not go unused—that is already wonderful. Still clearer is the end when we see how besides the furry animals of the Arctic there are also the seal, the walrus, and the whale which afford the inhabitants food from their flesh and warmth from their blubber. But the care of nature excites the greatest wonder when we see how she brings wood (though the inhabitants do not know whence it comes) to these barren climates, without which they would have neither canons, weapons, nor huts, and when we see how these natives are so occupied with their war against the animals that they live in peace with each other—but what drove them there was presumably nothing else than war.

The first instrument of war among the animals which man learned to tame and to domesticate was the horse (for the elephent belongs to later times, to the luxury of already established states). The art of cultivating certain types of plants (grain) whose original characteristics we do not know, and the increase and improvement of fruits by transplantation and grafting (in Europe perhaps only the crab apple and the wild pear), could arise only under conditions prevailing in already established states where property was secure. Before this could take place, it was necessary that men who had first subsisted in anarchic freedom by hunting, fishing and sheepherding should have been forced into an agricultural life. Then salt and iron were discovered. These were perhaps the first articles of commerce for the various peoples aad were sought far and wide; in this way a peaceful traffic among nations was established among the most distant peoples.

As nature saw to it that men could live everywhere in the world, she also despotically willed that they should do so, even against their inclination and without this ought being based on a concept of duty to which they were bound by a moral law. She chose war as the means to this end. So we see peoples whose common language shows that they have a common origin. For instance, the Samoyeds on the Arctic Ocean and a people with a similiar language a thousand miles away in the Altanian mountains are separated only by a Mongolian people adept at horsemanship and hence at war; the latter drove the former into the most inhospitable arctic regions where they certainly would not have spread of their own accord. Again, it is the same with the Finns who in the most northernly part of Europe are called Lapps; Goths and Sarmatians have separated them from the Hungarians to whom they are related in language. What can have driven the Eskimos, a race entirely distinct from all others in America and perhaps descended from primeval European adventurers, so far into the North, or the Prescherais as far south as Tierra del Fuego, if it were not war which nature uses to populate the whole earth ? War itself requires no special motive but appears to be engrafted on human nature; it passes even for something noble, to which the love of glory impels men quite apart from any selfish urges. Thus among the American savages, just as much as among those of Europe during the age of chivalry, military valour is held to be of great worth in itself, not only during war (which is natural) but in order that there should be war. Often war is waged only in order to show valour; thus an inner dignity is ascribed to war itself, and even some philosophers have praised it as an ennoblement of humanity, forgetting the pronouncement of the Greek who said, "War is an evil inasmuch as it produces more wicked men than it takes away." So much for the measures nature takes to lead the human race, considered as a class of animals, to her own end.

Now we come to the question concerning that which is most essential in the design of perpetual peace : What has nature done with regard to this end which man's own reason makes his duty ? That is, what has nature done to favour man's moral purpose, and how has she guaranteed (by compulsion but without prejudice to his freedom) that he shall do that which he ought to but does not do under the laws of freedom ? This question refers to all three phases of public law, namely, civil law, the law of nations, and the law of world citizenship. If I say of nature that she wills that this or that occur, I do not mean that she imposes a duty on us to do it, for this can be done only by free practical reason; rather I mean that she herself does it, whether we will or not.

1 Even if people were not forced by internal discord to submit to public laws, war would compel them to do so, for we have already seen that nature has placed each people near another which presses upon it, and against this it must form itself into a state in order to defend itself. Now the republican constitution is the only one entirely fitting to the rights of man. But it is the most difficult to establish and even harder to preserve, so that many say a repulic would have

to be a nation of angels, because men with their selfish inclinations are not capable of a constitution of such sublime form. But precisely with these inclinations nature comes to the aid of the general will established on reason, which is revered even though impotent in practice. Thus it is only a question of a good organization of the state (which does lie in man's power), whereby the powers of each selfish inclination are so arranged in opposition that one moderates or destroys the ruinous effect of the other. The consequence for reason is the same as if none of them existed, and man is forced to be a good citizen even if not a morally good person.

The problem of organizing a state, however hard it may seem, can be solved even for a race of devils, if only they are intelligent. The problem is : "Given a multitude of rational beings requiring universal laws for their preservation, but each of whom is secretly inclined to exempt himself from them, to establish a constitution in such a way that, although their private intentions conflict, they check each other with the result that their public conduct is the same as if they had no such intentions."

A problem like this must be capable of solution; it does not require that we know how to attain the moral improvement of men but only that we should know the mechanism of nature in order to use it on men, organizing the conflict of the hostile intentions present in a people in such a way that they must compel themselves to submit to coercive laws. Thus a state of peace is established in which laws have force. We can see, even in actual states, which are far from perfectly organized, that in their foreign relations they approach that which the idea of right prescribes. This is so in spite of the fact that the intrinsic element of morality is certainly not the cause of it. (A good constitution is not to be expected from morality, but, conversely, a good moral condition of a people is to be expected only under a good constitution.) Instead of genuine morality, the mechanism of nature brings it to pass through selfish inclinations, which naturally conflict outwardly but which can be used by reason as a means for its own end, the sovereignty of law, and, as concerns the state, for promoting and securing internal and external peace.

also the legislative authority which must be obeyed without argument...........

2. Si fecisti, nega. What you have committed, deny that it was your fault—for instance, that you have brought your people to despair and hence to rebellion. Rather assert that it was due to the obstinacy of your subjects; or, if you have conquered a neighbouring nation, say that the fault lies in the nature of man, who, if not met by force, can be counted on to make use of it to conquer you..............

Then it may be said, "Seek ye first the kingdom of pure practical reason and its righteousness, and your end (the blessing of perpetual peace) will necessarily follow." For it is the peculiarity of morals especially with respect to its principles of public law and hence in relation to a politics known a priori, that the less it makes conduct depend on the proposed end, i.e.. the intended material or moral advantage. the more it agrees with it in general. This is because it is the universal will given a priori (in a nation or in the relations among different, nations) which determines the law among men, and if practice consistently follows it, this will can also, by the mechanism of nature, cause the desired result and make the concept of law effective. So for instance, it is a principle of moral politics that a people should unite into a state according to juridical concepts of freedom and equality and this principal is based not on prudence but on duty. Political moralists may argue as much as they wish about the natural mechanism of a mass of men forming a society, assuming a mechanism which would weaken those principles and vitiate their end; or they may seek to prove their assertions by examples of poorly organized constitutions of ancient and modern times (for instance, of democracies without representative systems). They deserve no hearing, particularly as such a pernicious theory may itself occasion the evil which it prophesies, throwing human beings into one class with all other living machines, differing from them only in their consciousness that they are not free, which makes them, in their own judgment, the most miserable of all beings in the world...........

Even in his Recollections he has stated:

"......As I then believed that there was a little green stick whereon was written something which would destory all evil in men and give them great blessings, so I now believe that such truth exists among people and will be revealed to them and will give them what it promises."[2]

This very tendency of love grew in course of time in the form of love for humanity. He passed his Matriculation at the age of sixteen from Kazan University. Though he was a rich man, he somehow or the other became interested in military career and accordingly in 1851 got himself enlisted as a junker ("gentleman volunteer)" in the artillery section of Russian army. He got his commission after three years. At the time of the Crimean war, he was posted at Sevastopol. In the said war he exhibited his remarkable courage in the face of danger and death. Tolstoy had his writing habit even at that time. He wrote some stories and sketches describing the life during the siege of Sevastopol. They were so vivid and moving that even the Czar Alexander II was impressed by them and issued an order to guard his life.

Tolstoy resigned from the army in 1857. Thereafter he stayed in Moscow and led very loose life.

In the years 1859-60, however, Tolstoy visited Europe and had the opportunity of meeting great scholars. That had a very sobering effect. His life received a welcome change. He became a magistrate whose job was to settle land disputes. He also started a school for the children of farmers. He had this opinion that "natural lights" are better than "the artifical standards of civilisation"

Tolstoy has confessed in his confession that he "committed every crime in the calendar and yet was regarded by all as a comparatively moral man" in his youth.[3]

He married Sophia Behrs in September 1862. After his marriage, Tolstoy had some very nice domestic life for eleven

2. *Ibid.* p. 36
3. Count Leo N. Tolstoy. Latest Works. Life General Index Bibliography, translated by Leo Wiener, Dana Estes & Company, Boston. p. 240

years. In 1873 however his son Peter died suddenly. Thereafter his aunt died: These deaths were followed by deaths of his two more sons. These shocking events upset Tolstoy and he began to think about the problem of existence itself. According to his own version he was living on "the verge of suicide and despair." To forget his sorrows,he started living like common men who have " strength to live and die quietly and joyfully." He thought that their joyful life was because of their "strong lucid, unassailable faith". He visited monastries and churches. His efforts were rewarded. He began to understand the meaning of life, unaffected by death. But at the same time he noticed that external confession of faith was not always real. Most often it was deceptive.

Tolstoy's curiosity did not end here. He pursued the subject by making an intensive study of theology. He came to the conclusion that the faith professed by the organized church was "not only a lie but an immoral deception" and the church constituting the bulk of men asserting that they alone know truth is "the chief obstacle to christ's teaching being understood by the people." Christ has declared "Thou shalt not kill"; but the church aligns itself with the state and prays for the destruction of the enemy. Christ declared that the kingdom of God can be established on earth by the practice of the golden rule of universal brotherhood, but the church asserts that salvation can be attained only if the church rituals as a "symbol of atonement of the world's sins through the vicarious suffering of Christ" are strictly and blindly followed. Tolstoy therefore concluded that the "organised church was the greatest enemy of true Christianity". He made an attempt to study the Gospels in the original in order to grasp the true import of Christ's teachings. He came to the conclusion as a result of his thorugh study that Christ's true teaching was "Resist not evil". He wrote piercing works like "Criticism of Dogmatic Theology". "The Four Gospels, Harmonized are Translated, and" My Religion "or What I Believe". Tolostoy's critical works were not liked by the state and church authorities. His book "My Religion" was prohibited as soon as it was published in Russia.

In 1881 Tolstoy had an occasion to see the misery of slum-dwellers of Moscow. He was so much moved by the sight that he declared it to be a grave "crime" to live in luxury when people have to face such ignoble fate. He wrote "What shall we do then?" and established therein that the cause of poverty of the poor is to be found in the idleness of the rich. The rich deny body labour to themselves and appropriate the fruits of the labourers and producers through immoral means. He could understand why the poor doubted the intentions of the rich even behind their philanthrophic acts.

"I am sitting on a man's neck, choking him, and demanding that he carry me, and without getting off him, I assure myself and others that I am very sorry for him and want to alleviate his condition by all possible means except by getting off his neck." [4] This was the analysis of the situation by Tolstoy. He therefore advised the rich to get off from the necks of the poor.

Tolstoy denounced money because it was the modern form of slavery according to him. His conclusion was:

"Money is a new and terrible form of slavery, and like the old form of personal slavery, it corrupts both the slave and the slave-owner, but it is even much worse, because it frees the slave and the slave-owner from personal human relations.[5]"

One cannot abolish poverty by any amount of charity. Tolstoy was firm in his opinion that poverty can be eradicated only when everybody shall do some bodily work and teach even the poor to earn in that manner. Therefore "to do good it is not money that is needed, but first of all, the ability at least for a time to renounce the conventionalities of our life, not to be afraid to soil our boots and garments, nor to be afraid of bed bugs and nor lice, of typhoid, diphtheria, or smallpox; we must be able to sit down on the cot of a ragged fellow and talk with him so intimately that he will feel that the talker respects and loves him, and is not acting and admiring himself."[6]

People no doubt must join in a struggle against Nature because our mankind can wrest favours from Nature only in this

4. Count Leo N. Tolstoy, What Shall We Do Then?, translated by Leo Wiener, J.M. Dent & Co., London, p. 15
5. *Idid.* p. 124 and p. 164
6. *Idid.* p. 349

manaer. If we do not struggle against Nature, we may be required to Starve.

"Love cannot be stupid. As love for one man would not let us read novels to him who was starving, or hang costly earrings on him who was naked, so love for mankind will not let us serve it by amusing the willed while we leave the cold and hungry to die of want.

True love, love not merely in words but in deeds, cannot be stupid—it is the one thing giving true perception and wisdom.

And, therefore, a man penetrated by love will make a mistake, but will be sure to do first what love of man first requires; he will do what maintains the life of the hungry, the cold and the heavy-laden, and that is all done by a direct struggle with nature."[7]

Art, according to Tolstoy, too must serve humanity. True art had no meaning "except as an expression about the destiny and the good of man".[8] The artist and thinker must be self-effacing, must care a fig for their personal interests. The good of humanity is their own good. "Self-renunciation and suffering will be the share of the thinker and the artist, because his aim is the good of men. Men are unhappy; they suffer, they perish, There is no time for waiting and taking things coolly.

The thinker and artist will never sit on Olympian heights, as we are accustomed to think; he will always, eternally, be agitated and disturbed"[9]

According to Tolstoy "Not he will be a thinker and an artist who is educated in an establishment, where they make a scholar and an artist...and receives a diploma and a competency; but he who would be glad to refrain from thinking and expressing what is implanted in his soul, and yet is unable to refrain from doing that toward which he is drawn by two insuperable forces – by his inner necessity and by the demands of men".[10]

7. Leo Tolstoy, Essays and Letters, translated by A. Maude, Oxford University Press, London, pp. 11-12

8. What Snall We Do Then?, p. 279

9. *Ibid*, p. 285

10. *Ibid*

Tolstoy led a life that was true to his inner conviction. He became a changed man. He began to live and dress like a peasant; he did not require any servant; he cleaned his own room, washed his clothes himself. He chopped firewood and brought water to the household from a well. He learnt boot-making and even persuaded his daughter to use shoes prepared by him. He gave up hunting, drinking of wine and eating meat. He also left tobacco and even tea was discarded by him. He even started ploughing the land. His love for bodily labour is thus very evident.

But his pacifist tendencies got stimulation from the reading of literature of pacifists like William Lloyed Garrison and M. Adin Ballon of the U.S.A. He also got stimulation from the Doukhobors—belonging to the pacifist sect of Russian Christians. These Russian pacifists refused to serve in the army on the religious and conscientious grounds. Police was very hard on those who refused to serve in the army or even showed any sympathy for the pacifists. Some of Tolostoy's friends became subjects of such ruthless behaviour. Birukoff and Chertkov who were so close to Tolstoy were banished to Siberia because of their pacifistic activities.

Tolstoy opposed the crude prevalent trend of Christianity. He was a man filled with spirirual potentiality and could find out the truth that the real teaching of Christ has been forgotten by his so-called followers and the intersted persons carried out their ugly trade of misleading people in the name of religion and getting their selfish ends served. The tradition-loving church therefore never forgave him for declaring truth from the house-tap. The Holy Synod's Edict excommunicated him in 1901. And Tolstoy gave them befitting reply by declaring: "I began by loving my Orthodox faith more than my peace, then I loved Christianity more than my Church, and now I love truth more than anything in the world."[11]

He was of the opinion that main cause of prevention of Christian faith was the fact that people had this irrational opinion that they could accept the teaching of Christ without

11. Leo Tolstoy, Essays and Letters, p. 287

changing their old traditional ways of conduct and habit. We find a verse in St. John that states "And men loved darkness rather than light because their deeds were evil". Hence the reformation that should have come through the acceptance of Christian faith never came. The old bad habits continue to dominate and the people continued to walk their trodden path, even though ostensibly they accepted Christanity.

Though this has actually happened, yet sometimes human rationality tells people that though they profess to follow Christ, they are actually drifting away from his teaching. They became sometimes aware of the contradiction between what Christ told them to follow and what they actually do.

It happened even in other fields of life. Human rationality tells a man that all human beings are brothers and all have equal rights. But at the same time human society continues to be divided into the age-long divisions of haves and have-nots.

In the domain of political life things are still worse. The state is not meant for loosing a reign of terror and compelling people to help it in the perpetration of crimes of group murders in the name of war, and yet people bow before the state and accept even the most irrational and immoral commands to save their skin.

Tolstoy was of the opinion that historically mankind is moving in the direction of gradual evolution. The first stage was the stage of the individual or animal. The second stage was the stage of the social or pagan. And the third stage that has to appear will be the divine or universal stage. In the first stage man remains individual and gratifies his desires in a most selfish manner. He is a savage. In the second stage man associates himself with family, the race and finally with the state. But in the third stage man's life shall [become wide enough. He shall not remain a selfish savage. Nor shall he remain tied down to the family, the race, or the state even. He shall be a universal man since he shall love God alone.

The trouble with our age is that the world is still in the second stage. The state has become too strong because the restraints have been thrown away. The masses have more morality than the state. Tolstoy declared, The whole history of two thousand years consists of this alteration of relations between the moral development of the masses and demoralisation of all the governments."[12]

From this fact Tolstoy deduced the inference that violence must become more widespread as a result of this situation.

"The evil of violence, passing into the hands of a government, always tends to increase and become greater than that which it is supposed to destroy, while it becomes less necessary as the tendency to use violence among the individual members of society progressively diminishes." writes Tolstoy. He further adds: "Governmental power, even if it suppresses private violence, always introduces fresh forms of violence into the lives of men and does this increasingly as it continues and grows stronger."[13]

The government is essentially based on force at the present moment of history. Government uses this force to compel those who oppose it, to obey its commands. The army is so organised that it will blindly obey the command of the authority. This is done by every government. And many times the increase in the army and the armaments mainly for utilizing them for internal peace by the State is misunderstood by the neighbouring state as a preparation of war. The neighbouring state too, therefore starts the process of increase of army and armaments. The violent race thus begins. Tolstoy's analysis runs on this line of thinking.

"The increase of armies arises simultaneously from two causes, each of which reciprocally evokes the other; armies are needed both against enemies at home and to maintain the position of a state against its neighbours. The one conditions the other. The despotism of a government at home increases in proportion to the increase and strengthening of its army and its external successes; and the aggressiveness of governments grows in proportion to the increase of their internal despotism."[14] It is said irony of fate that the states that

12. Count Leo Tolstoy, The Kingdom of God and Peace Essays, translated by Aylmer Maude, Oxford University Press, London, p. 202
13. *Ibid.* p. 203
14. *Ibid.* p. 209

were established to protect people, shirk their reponsibility and throw people into the ocean of destruction.

Tolstoy seems to be perfectly right when he writes :

"Governments were to free men from the cruelty of individual strife, to give them security in the performance of a groug life. But instead of that they subject men to the same necessity of strife, merely substituting strife with other States for strife with individual neighbours, and the danger of destruction both for the individual and for the State they leave just as it was."[15]

Tolstoy was convinced that violence and war cannot be abolished by adopting resolutions affirming faith in peace. These resolutions are nothing more than scrapes of paper. The only way of destroying this bloody trail of wars is to withdraw every cooperation from the state that represents violence and makes every citizen an accomplice in the various acts of ignoble violence. The machinery of government is so cunningly designed and it contains so many "instigators, participants and abettors" that no single person feels himself morally responsible for the perpetration of those crimes. "As in a wicker basket all the ends are so carefully interwoven that they cannot be seen, so is it with the responsibility for crime. Individual responsibilities are so manipulated that no man perceives precisely what he is incurring."[16]

The murderers very cunningly compel all the witnesses to strike the body of the victim "with a view to dividing the responsibility among the greatest number possible." They try to involve as many fellow citizens as possible in the perpetration of the crime. It is really a verywell-planned scheme. "Some demand the crime, some propose it, some determine it, some confirm it, some order it, some execute it."[17] The point to be noted is that though so man participate in the commission of a crime, but practically every one of the cla[illegible] participants thinks that responsibility for the [illegible] belongs to some one-else and he himself has [illegible] nothing immoral. The demoralis-

15. *Ibid.* p. 210
16. Count Leo Tolstoy, The Kingdom of God is Within You, p. 327
17. *Ibid.* p. 327

ing influence of these persons is more abnoxious and harmful than the acts of cheats and robbers.

"Thieves, robbers, murderers, rogues, who commit acts which they themselves, as well as other men, know to be evil, serve as a warning to show men what is evil, and make them hate it. Those, however, who steal, rob, torture, and murder, justifying themselves by pretended religious, scientific, or other motives, like the landowners, merchants, factory-owners and government servants of the present time, by provoking imitation, injure not only their victim but thousands and millions of men who are corrupted by their influence and who become so blinded that they cannot distinguish the difference between good and evil.

One fortune acquired......in any of these ways, not only permitted, but approved by the leaders of society, when furthermore, it is supported by a show of charity, surely demoralises men more than millions thefts, frauds, or robberies—sins committed against the laws of the land and subject to judicial prosecution."[18]

Men cannot make the path of real peace smooth by participating in the acts of the state in some way or the other. Unless they make it a point to dissociate themselves from the acts and fruits of the state and bring about a revolution in their mental outlook, the things shall continue to remain as they are.

It is evident that Tolstoy's thinking was clear and constructive. Our modern age can certainly derive some worth-while advantage by giving attention to his thoughts.

Tolstoy died on 7th November, 1910. He was a free thinker and had been very critical about the Holy Church, the official church. The Synod forbade all memorial services as a mark of its opposition to Tolstoy's untraditional thinking. But his personality was taller than the Syond itself. His death was mourned by the people of Russia. The St. Petersburg University remained closed in his honour. Even the theatres suspended their shows, and the Czar, the Dumas and the Council of State sent official messages of condolences. He was buried by the side of his beloved brother Nikolai's tomb.

18. *Ibid*, pp. 351-52

PATRIOTISM AND GOVERNMENT

The time is fast approaching when to call a man a patriot will be the deepest insult you can offer him. Patriotism now means advocating plunder in the interests of privileged classes of the particular State system into which we have happened to be born'.

—*E. Belfort Bax*

I have already several times expressed the thought that in our day the feeling of patriotism is an unnatural, irrational and harmful feeling, and a cause of a great part of the ills from which mankind is suffering; and that, consequently, this feeling should not be cultivated, as is now being done, but should, on the contrary, be suppressed and eradicated by all means available to rational men. Yet, strange to say—though it is undeniable that the universal armaments and destructive wars which are ruining the peoples result from that one feeling—all my arguments showing the backwardness, anachronism, and harmfulness of patriotism have been met, and are still met, either by silence, by intentional misinterpretation, or by a strange unvarying reply to the effect that only bad patriotism (Jingoism, or Chauvinism) is evil, but that real good patriotism is a very elevated moral feeling, to condemn which is not only irrational but wicked.

What this real, good patriotism consists in, we are never told; or, if anything is said about it, instead of explanation we get declamatory inflated phrases, or finally, some other conception is substituted for patriotism—something which has nothing in common with the patriotism we all know, and from the results of which we all suffer so severely. It is generally said that the real, good patriotism consists in desiring for one's own people or State such real benefits as do not infringe well-being of other nations.

Talking recently to an Englishman about the present war (viz. the South African War of 1899-1902), I said to him that the real cause of the war was not avarice, as people generally say, but patriotism, as is evident from the temper of the whole English society. The Englishman did not agree with me, and said that even were the case so, it resulted from the fact that the patriotism at present inspiring Englishmen is a bad patriotism; but that good patriotism, such as be was imbued with, would cause Englishmen, compatriots, to act well.

'Then do you wish only Englishmen to act well?' I asked.

'I wish all men to do so', said he; indicating clearly by that reply the characteristic of true benefits—whether moral, scientific, or even material and practical—which is that they spread out to all men. But, evidently, to wish such benefits to everyone, not only is not patriotic, but is the reverse of patriotic.

Neither do the peculiarities of each people constitute patriotism, though these things are purposely substituted for the conception of patriotism by its defenders. They say that the peculiarities of each people are an essential condition of human progress, and that patriotism, which seeks to maintain those peculiarities, is, therefore, a good and useful feeling. But is it not quite evident that if, once upon a time, these peculiarities of each people—these customs, creeds, languages—were conditions necessary for the life of humanity, in our time these same peculiarities form the chief obstacle to what is already recognised as an ideal—the brotherly union of the peoples? And therefore the maintenance and defence of any nationality—Russian, German, French, or Anglo-Saxon, provoking the corresponding maintenance and defence not only of Hungarian, Polish, and Irish nationalities, but also of Basque. Provencal, Mordva, Tchouvash, and many other nationalities—serves not to harmonize and unite men, but to estrange and divide them more and more from one another.

So that not the imaginary but the real patriotism, which we all know, by which most people today are swayed and from which humanity suffers so severely, is not the wish for spiritual benefits for one's own people (it is impossible to desire spiritual benefits for one's own people only), but is a very definite feeling of preference for one's own peoples and States, and a consequent wish to get for that people or State the greatest advantages and power that can be got—things which are obtainable only at the expense of the advantages and power of other peoples of States.

It would, therefore, seem obvious that patriotism as a feeling is bad and harmful, and as a doctrine is stupid. For it is clear that if each people and each State considers itself the best of peoples and States, they all live in a gross and harmful delusion.

II

One would expect the harmfulness and irrationality of patriotism to be evident to everybody. But the surprising fact is that cultured and learned men not only do not themselves notice the harm and stupidity of patriotism, but they resist every exposure of it with the greatest obstinacy and ardour (though without any rational grounds), and continue to belaud it as beneficent and elevating.

What does this mean?

Only one explanation of this amazing fact present itself to me.

All human history, from the earliest time to our own day, may be considered as a movement of the consciousness, both of individuals and of homogeneous groups, from lower ideas to higher ones.

The whole path travelled both by individuals and homogeneous groups may be represented as a consecutive flight of steps from the lowest, on the level of animal life, to the highest attained by the consciousness of man at a given moment of history.

Each man, like each separate homogeneous group, nation, or State, always moved and moves up this ladder of ideas. Some portions of humanity are in front, others lag behind, others, again—the majority—move somewhere between the most advanced and most backward. But all, whatever stage they may have reached, are inevitably and irresistibly moving from lower to higher ideas. And always, at any given moment, both the individuals and the separate groups of people—advanced, middle, or backward—stand in three different relations to the three stages of ideas amid which they move.

Always, both for the individual and for the separate groups of people, there are the ideas of the past, which are worn-out and have become strange to them, and to which they cannot revert; as for instance, in our Christian world, the ideas of annihalism, universal plunder, the rape of wives, and other customs of which only a record remains.

And there are the ideas of the present, instilled into men's minds by education, by example, and by the general activity of all around them; ideas under the power of which they live at a given time: for instance, in our own day, the ideas of property, State organization, trade, utilization of domestic animals, etc.

And there are the ideas of the future, of which some are already approaching realization and are obliging people to change their way of life and to struggle against the former ways: such ideas in our world as those of freeing the labourers, of giving equality to women, of disusing flesh food, etc.; while others, though already recognized, have not yet come into practical conflict with the old forms of life: such in our times are the ideas (which are we call ideals) or the extermination of violence, the arrangement of communal system of property, of a universal religion, and of a general brotherhood of men.

And. therefore, every man and every homogeneous group of men, on whatever level they may stand, having behind them worn-out remembrances of the past, and before them the ideals of the future, are always in a state of struggle between the moribund ideas of the present and the ideas of the future that are coming to life. It usually happens that when an idea which has been useful and even necessary in the past becomes superfluous, that idea, after a more or less prolonged struggle, yields its place to a new idea which was till then an ideal, but which thus becomes a present idea.

But it does occur that an antiquated idea, already replaced in people's consciousness by a higher one, is of such a kind that its maintenance is profitable to those people who have the greatest influence in their society. And then it happens that this antiquated idea, though it is in sharp contradiction to the whole surrounding form of life, which has been altering in other respects, continues to influence people and to sway their actions. Such retention of antiquated ideas always has occurred, and still occur, in the region of religion. The cause is, that the priests, whose profitable positions are bound up with the antiquated religious idea, purposely use their power to hold people to this antiquated idea.

The same thing occurs, and for similar reasons, in the political sphere, with reference to the patriotic idea, on which all arbitrary power is based. People to whom it is profitable to do so, maintain that idea by artificial means, though it now lacks both sense and utility. And as these people possess the most powerful means of influencing others, they are able to achieve their object.

In this, it seems to me, lies explanation of the strange contrast, between the antiquated patriotic idea, and that whole drift of ideas making in a contrary direction, which have already entered into the consciousness of the Christian World.

III

Patriotism, as a feeling of exclusive love for one's own people, and as a doctrine of the virtue of sacrificing one's tranquility, one's property, and even one's life, in defence of one's own people from slaughter and outrage by their enemies, was the highest idea of the period when each nation considered it feasible and just, for its own advantage, to subject to slaughter and outrage the people of other nations. But already some 2,000 years ago, humanity, in the person to the high-representatives of its wisdom, began to recognise the higher idea of a brotherhood of man; and that idea, penetrating man's consciousness more and more, has in our time attained most varied forms of realization. Thanks to improved means of communication, and to the unity of industry, of trade, of the arts, and of science, men are today so bound one to another that the danger of conquest, massacre, or outrage by a neighbouring people, has quite disappeared, and all peoples (the peoples, but not the Governments) live together in peaceful, mutually advantageous, and friendly commercial, industrial, artistic, and scientific relations, which they have no need and no desire to disturb. One would think, therefore, that the antiquated feeling of patriotism—being superflucus and incompatible with the consciousness we have reached of the existence of brotherhood among men of different nationalities—should dwindle more and more until it completely disappears. Yet the very opposite of this occurs: this harmful and antiquated feeling not only continues to exist, but burns more and more fiercely.

The peoples, without any reasonable ground, and contrary alike to their conception of right and to their own advantage, not only sympathize with Governments in their attacks on other nations, in their seizures of foreign possessions, and in defending by force what they have already stolen, but even themselves demand attacks, seizures, and defences: are glad of them, and take pride in them. The small oppressed nationalities which have fallen under the power of the great States—the Poles, Irish, Behemians, Finns or Armenians—resenting the patriotism of their conquerors, which is the cause of their oppression, catch from them the infection of their feeling of patriotism—which has ceased to be necessary, and is now obsolete, unmeaning, and harmful—and catch it to such a degree that all their activity is concentrated upon it, and they, themselves suffering from the patriotism of the stronger nations, are ready, for the sake of patriotism, to perpetrate on other peoples the same deeds that their oppressors have perpetrated and are perpetrating on them.

This occurs because the ruling classes (including not only the actual rulers with their officials, but all the classes who enjoy an exceptionally advantageous position: the capitalists, journalists, and most of the artists and scientists) can retain their position—exceptionally advantageous in comparison with that of the labouring masses—thanks only to the Government organization, which rests on patriotism. They have in their hands all the most powerful means of influencing the people, and always sedulously support patriotic feelings in themselves and in others, more especially as those feelings which uphold the Government's power are those that are always best rewarded by that power. Every official prospers the more in his career, the more patriotic he is; so also the army man gets promotion in time of war—the war is produced by patriotism.

Patriotism and its result—wars—give enormous revenue to the newspaper trade, and profits to many other trades. Every writer, teacher and professor is more secure in his place the more he preaches patriotism. Every Emperor and King obtains the more fame the more he is addicted to patriotism.

The ruling classes have in their hands the army, money, the schools, the churches, and the press. In the schools they kindle patriotism in the children by means of histories describing their own people as the best of all peoples and always right. Among adults they kindle it by spectacles, jubilees, monuments, and by a laying patriotic press. Above all, they inflame patriotism in this way: perpetrating every kind of injustice and harness against other nations, they provoke in them enmity towards their own people, and then in turn exploit that enmity to embitter their people against the foreigner.

V

The intensification of this terrible feeling of patriotism has gone on among the European peoples in a rapidly increasing progression, and in our time has reached the utmost limits, beyond which there is no room for it to extend.

Within the memory of people not yet old, an occurrence took place showing most obviously the amazing intoxication caused by patriotism among the people of Christendom.

The ruling classes of Germany excited the patriotism of the masses of their people to such a degree that, in the second half of the nineteenth century, a law was proposed in accordance with which all the men had to become soldiers: all the sons, husbands, fathers, learned men, and godly men, had to learn to murder, to become submissive slaves of those above them in military rank, and be absolutely ready to kill whomsoever they were ordered to kill; to kill men of oppressed nationalities, and their own working—men standing up for their rights, and even their rights, and even their own fathers and brothers—as was publicly proclaimed by that most impudent of potentates, William II.

The horrible measure, outraging all man's best feelings in the grossest manner, was, under the influence of patriotism, acquiesced in without murmur by the people of Germany. It resulted in their victory over the French. That victory yet further excited the patriotism of Germany, and, by reaction, that of France, Russia, and the other Powers; and the men of European countries unresistingly submitted to the introduction of general military service—i.e., to a state of slavery involving a degree of humiliation and submission incomparably worse than any slavery of the ancient world. After this servile submission of the masses to the calls of patriotism, the audacity, cruelty, and insanity of the Governments knew no bounds. A competition in the usurpation of other people's lands in Asia, Africa and America began—evoked partly by whim, partly by vanity, and partly by covetousness—and accompanied by ever greater distrust and enmity between the Governments.

The destruction of the inhabitants on the lands seized was accepted as a quite natural proceeding. The only question was, who should be first in seizing other people's land and destroying the inhabitants?

All the Governments not only most evidently infringed, and are infringing, the elementary demands of justice in relation to the conquered people, and in relation to one another, but they were guilty, and continue to be guilty, of every kind of cheating, swindling, bribing, fraud, spying, robbery, and murder; and the peoples not only sympathized, and still sympathize, with them in all this, but they rejoice when it is their own Government and not another Government that commits such crimes.

The mutual enmity between the different peoples and State has reached latterly, such amazing dimensions that, notwithstanding the fact that there is no reason why one State should attack another, everyone knows, that all the Governments stand with their claws out and showing their teeth, and only waiting for someone to be in trouble, or become weak, in order to tear him to pieces with as little risk as possible.

All the peoples of the so called Christian World have been reduced by patriotism to such a state of brutality, that not only those who are obliged to kill or be killed desire slaughter and rejoice in murder, but all the people of Europe and America, living peaceably in their homes exposed to no danger, are, at each war, thanks to easy means of communication and to the press—in the position of the spectators in a Roman circus, and like them delight in the slaugethr, and raise the bloodthirsty cry, 'Pollice verso.'

Not adults only, but also children, pure, wise children, rejoice, according to their nationality, when they hear that the number killed and lacerated by lyddite or other shells on some particular day was not 700 but 1,000 Englishmen or Boers.

And parents (I know such cases) encourage their children in such brutality.

But that is not all. Every increase in the army of one nation (and each nation, being in danger, seeks to increase its army for patriotic reason) obliges its neighbours to increase their armies, also from patriotism, and this evokes a fresh increase by the first nation.

And the same thing occurs with fortifications and navies; one State has built ten ironclads, a neighbour builds eleven; then the first builds twelve, and so on to infinity.

'I'll pinch you.' 'And I'll punch your head.' 'And I'll stab you with a dagger.' (And I'll bludgeon you.' 'And I'll shoot you.'... Only bad children, drunken men, or animals, quarrel or fight so, but yet it is just what is going on among the highest representatives of the most enlightened Governments, the very men who undertake to direct the education and the morality as their subjects.

V

The position is becoming worse and worse, and there is no stopping this descent towards evident perdction.

The one way of escape believed in by credulous people has now been closed by recent events. I refer to the Hague Conference, and to the war between England and the Transvaal which immediately followed it.

If people who think little, or but superficially, were able to comfort themselves with the idea that international courts of arbitration would supersede wars and ever-increasing armaments, the Hague Conference and the war that followed it demonstrated in the most palpable manner the impossibility of finding a solution of the difficulty in that way. After the Hague Conference, it became obvious that as long as Governments with armies exist, the termination of armaments and of wars is impossible. That an agreement should become possible, it is necessary that the parties to it should trust each other. And in order that the Powers should trust each other, they must lay down their arms, as is done by the bearers of a flag of truce when they meet for a conference.

So long as Governments, distrusting one another, not only do not disband or decrease their armies, but always increase them in correspondence with augmentation made by their neighbours, and by means of spies watch every movement of troops, knowing that each of the Powers will attack its neighbour as soon as it sees its way to do so, no agreement a is possible, and every conference is either a stupidity, or pastime, or a fraud, or an impertinence, or all of these together.

It was particularly becoming for the Russian rather than any other Government to be the enfant terrible of the Hague Conference. No one at home being allowed to reply to all its evidently mendacious manifestations and rescripts, the Russian Government is so spoilt, that—having without the least scruple ruined its own people with armaments, strangled Poland, plundered Turkestan and China, and being specially engaged in suffocating Finland—it proposed disarmament to the Governments, in full assurance that it would be trusted.

But strange, unexpected and indecent as such a proposal was—especially at the very time when orders were being given to increase its army—the words publicly uttered in the hearing of the people were such that for the sake of appearances the Governments of the other Powers could not decline the comical and evidently insincere consultation; and so the delegates met—knowing in advance that nothing would come of it—and for several weeks (during which they drew good salaries) though they were laughing in their sleeves, they all conscientiously pretended to be much occupied in arranging peace among the nations.

The Hague Conference, followed up as it was by the terrible bloodshed of the Transvaal War, which no one attempted, or is now attempting, to stop, was, nevertheless, of some use, though not at all in the way expected of it—it was useful because it showed in the most obvious manner that the evils from which the peoples are suffering cannot be cured by Governments. That Governments, even if they wished to, can terminate neither armaments nor wars.

Governments, to have a reason for existing, must defend

their people from other people's attack. But not one people wishes to attack, or does attack, another. And therefore Governments, for from wishing for pcace, carefully excite the anger of other nations against themselves. And having excited other people's anger against themselves, and stirred up the patriotism of their own people, each Government then assures its people that it is in danger and must be defended.

And having the power in their hands, the Governments can both irritate other nations and excite patriotism at home, and they carefully do both the one and the other; nor can they act otherwise, for their existence depends on thus acting.

If, in former times, Governments were necessary to defend their people from other people's attacks, now, on the contrary, Governments artificially disturb the peace that exists between the nations, and provoke enmity among them.

When it was necessary to plough in order to sow, ploughing was wise; but evidently it is absurd and harmful to go on ploughing after the seed has been sown. But this is just what the Governments are obliging their people to do: to infringe the unity which exists, and which nothing would infringe if it were not for the Governments.

VI

In reality what are these Governments, without which people think they could not exist.

There may have been a time when such Governments were necessary, and when the evil of supporting a Government was less then that of being defenceless against organized neighbours; but now such Governments have become unnecessary, and are a far greater evil than all the dangers with which they frighten their subjects.

Not only military Governments, but Governments in general, could be, I will not say useful, but at least harmless, only if they consisted of immaculate, holy people, as is theoretically the case among the Chinese. But then Governments, by the nature of their activity, which consists in committing acts of violence, are always composed of elements the most contrary to holiness—of the most audacious, unscrupulous, and perverted people.

A Government, therefore, and especially a Government entrusted with military power, is the most dangerous organization possible.

The Government, in the widest sense, including capitalists and the Press, is nothing else than an organization which places the greater part of the people in the power of a smaller part, who dominate them; that smaller part is subject to a yet smaller part, and that again to a yet smaller, and so on, reaching at last a few people, or one single man, who by means of military force has power over all the rest. So that all this organization resembles a cone, of which all the parts are completely in the power of those people, or of that one person, who happen to be at the apex.

The apex of the cone is seized by those who are more cunning, audacious, and unscrupulous than the rest, or by someone who happens to be the heir of those who were audacious and unscrupulous.

To-day it may be Boris Godunof, and tomorrow Gegory Otrepyef. Today the licentious Catherine, who with her paramours has murdered her husband; tomarrow Pougatchef; then Paul the madman, Nicholas I., or Alexander III.

To-day it may be Napoleon, tomarrow a Bourbon or an Orleans, a Boulanger or a Panama Company; to-day it may be Gladstone, tomorrow Salisbury, Chamberlain, or Rhodes.

And to such Governments is allowed full power, not only over property and lives, but even over the moral developments, the education, and the religious guidance of everybody.

People construct such a terrible machine of power, they allow any one to seize it who can (and the chances always are that it will be seized by the most morally worthless)—they slavishly submit to him, and are then surprised that evil comes of it. They are afraid of Anarchists' bombs, and are not afraid of this terrible organization which is always threatening them with the greatest calamities.

People found it useful to themselves together in order to resist their enemies, as the Circassians did when resisting attacks. But the danger is quite past, and yet people go on tying themselves together.

They carefully tie themselves up so that one man can have

them all at his mercy; then they throw away the end of the rope that ties them, and leave it trailing for some rascal or fool to seize and to do them whatever harm he likes.

Really, what are people doing but just that—when they set up, submit to, and maintain an organized and military Government ?

VII

To deliver men from the terrible and ever-increasing evils of armaments and wars, we want neither congresses nor conferences, nor treaties, nor courts of arbitration, but the destruction of those instruments of violence which are called Governments, and from which humanity's greatest evils flow.

To destroy Governmental violence, only one thing is needed: it is that people should understand that the feeling of patriotism, which alone supports that instrument of violence, is a rude, harmful, disgraceful, and bad feeling, and, above all, is immoral. It is a rude feeling, because it is one natural only to people standing on the lowest level of morality, and expecting from other nations such outrages as they themselves are ready to inflict; it is a harmful feeling, because it disturbs advantageous and joyous, peaceful relations with other peoples, and above all, produces that Governmental organization under which power may fall, and does fall, into the hands of the worst men; it is a disgraceful feeling, because it turns man not merely into a slave, but into a fighting cock, a bull, or a gladiator, who wastes his strength and his life for objects which are not his own but his Governments; and it is an immoral feeling, because, instead of confessing one's self a son of God (as Christianity teaches us) or even a free man guided by his own reason. each man under the influence of patriotism confesses himself the son of his fatherland and the slave of his Government, and commits actions contrary to his reason and his conscience.

It is only necessary that people should understand this, and the terrible bond, called Government, by which we are chained together, will fall to pieces of itself without struggle; and with it will cease the terrible and useless evils it produces.

And people are already beginning to understand this. This,

We will pay no paw rents, no tithes to your sham sharities, and we will speak our minds upon occasion.

'We will educate men.

'And all the time our silent influence will be going out, and even the men who are conscripted will be half-hearted and refuse to fight. We will educate men into the thought that the Christ Life of Peace and Goodwill is better than the Life of Strife, Bloodshed, and War.

'"Peace on Earth."—it can only come when men do away with armies, and are willing to do unto other men ast hey would be done by.'

So writes a citizen of the United States; and from various sides, in various forms, such voices are sounding.

This is what a German soldier writes;

'I went through two campaigns with the Prussian Guards (in 1866 and 1870), and hate war from the bottom of my soul, for it has made me inexpressibly unfortunate. We wounded soldiers generally receive such a miserable recompense that we have indeed to be ashamed of having once been patriots. I, for instance, get nine pence a day for my right arm, which was shot through at the attack on St. Privat, August 18, 1870. Some hunting dogs have more allowed for their keep, And I have suffered for years from my twice wounded arm. Already in 1866 I took part in the War against Austria, and fought at Trautenau and Koniggratz, and saw horrors enough. In 1870, being in the reserve I was called out again; and, as I have already said, I was wounded in the attack at St. Privat: my right arm was twice shot through lengthwise. I had to leave a good place in a brewery, and was unable afterwards to regain it. Since then I have never been able to get on my feet again. The intoxication soon passed, and there was nothing left for the wounded invalid but to keep himself, alive on a beggarly pittance eked out my charity. . . .

'In a world in which people run round like trained animals, and are not capable of any other idea than that of over-reaching one another for the sake of mammon—in such a world let people think me a crank; but, for all that, I feel in myself the divine idea of peace, which is so beautifully expressed in the Sermon on the Mount. My deepest conviction is that war is only trade on a larger scale—the ambitious and powerful trade with the happiness of the peoples.

'And what horrors do we not suffer from it. Never shall I forget the pitiful groans that pierced one to the marrow.

'People who never did each other any harm begin to slaughter one another like wild animals, and petty, slavish souls—implicate the good God, making Him their confederate in such deeds.

'My neighbour in the ranks had his jaw broken by a bullet. The poor wretch went wild with pain. He ran like a madman, and in the scorching summer heat could not even get water to cool his horrible wound. Our Commander, the Crown Prince (who was afterwards the noble Emperor Frederick wrote in his diary: "War—is an irony on the Gospels."

People are beginning to understand the fraud of patriotism, in which all the Governments take such pains to keep them involved.

VIII

' But, it is usually asked, 'what will there be instead of Governments?'

There will be nothing. Something that has long been useless, and therefore superfluous and bad, will be abolished. An organ that, being unnecessary, has become harmful, will be abolished.

'But, people generally say, 'if there is no Government, people will violate and kill each other.'

Why? Why should the abolition of the organization which arose in consequence of violence, and which has been handed down from generation to generation to do violence—why should the abolition of such an organization now devoid of use, cause people to outrage and kill one another? On the contrary, the presumption is that the abolition of the organ of violence would result in people ceasing to violate and kill one another.

Now, some men are specially educated and trained to kill and to do violence to other people—there are men who are and no one will help you to stop it or to prevent it, if you do not help yourselves.

And there is only one kind of help possible—it lies in the abolition of that terrible linking up into a cone of violence, which enables the person or persons who succeed in seizing the apex to have power over all the rest, and to hold that power the more firmly the more cruel and inhuman they are, as we see by the cases of the Napoleons, Nicholas I., Bismarck, Chamberlain, Rhodes, and our Russian Dictators who rule the people in the Tsar's name.

And there is only one way to destrory this binding together —it is by shaking off the hypnotism of patriotism.

Understand that all the evils from which you suffer, you yourselves cause by yielding to the suggestions by which Emperors, Kings, Members of Parliament, Governors, officers, capitalists, priests, authors, artists, and all who need this fraud of patriotism in order to live upon your labour, deceive you.

Whoever you may be—Frenchman, Russian, Pole, Englishman, Irishman, or Bohemian—understand that all your real human interests, whatever they may be—agricultural, industrial, commercial, artistic, or scientific—as well as your pleasures and joys, in no way run counter to the interests of other peoples or States; and that you are united, by mutual co-operation, by interchange of services, by the joy of wide brotherly intercourse, and by the interchange not merely of goods but also of thoughts and feelings, with the folk of other lands.

Understand that the question as to who manages to seize Wei-hai-wei, Port Arthur, or Cuba—your Government or another—does not affect you, or, rather, that every such seizure made by your Government injures you, by inevitably bringing in its train all sorts of pressure on you by your Government to force you to take part in the robbery and violence by which alone such seizures are made, or can be retained when made. Understand that your life can in no way be bettered by Alsace becoming German or French, and Ireland or Poland being free or enslaved—whoever holds them. You are free to live where you will, if even you be an Alsatian, an Irishman or Pole. Understand, too, that by stirring up patriotism you will only make the case worse, for the subjection in which your people are kept has resulted simply from the struggle between patriotisms, and every manifestation of patriotism in one nation provokes a corresponding reaction in another. Understand that salvation from your woes is only possible when you free yourself from the obsolete idea of patriotism and from the obedience to Government that is, based upon it, and when boldly enter into the region of that higher idea, the brotherly union of the peoples, which has long since come to life, and from all sides is calling you to itself.

If people would but understand that they are not the sons of some fatherland or other, nor of Governments, but are sons of God, and can therefore neither be slaves nor enemies one to another—those insane, unnecessary, worn-out, pernicious organizations called Governments, and all the sufferings, violations, humiliations, and crimes which they occasion, would cease.

May 10, 5, 1900

INDEX